MW01226016

U^{THE}PWARD SPIRAL

A Primer for Supervisors

*How to Create a Workplace Where You'll Leave a
Legacy of Competent, Committed Employees*

T. GARY CURTIS

Copyright 2013 by T. Gary Curtis

All rights reserved. No part of this book may be used or reproduced in any manner without the written permission of the author except in the case of brief quotations in articles or reviews.

Published by:
The Upward Spiral Company, LLC
120 Sand Piper Loop
Helena, Montana 59602

Book design by: Shellee Nolan, Eagle Printing & Graphic Design, Richland, Washington

ISBN: 978-0-615-92501-1
Printed in the United States of America

Praise for the Upward Spiral

"Gary Curtis taught and influenced a whole generation of managers in Montana. The lessons and techniques I learned from him still serve me today; I use them in my business and civic organizations I belong to, and in the House of Representatives. If you want down-to-earth, practical strategies to make your organization more effective, more productive, and working better as a team, read and practice what Gary has to say in this book."
Chuck Hunter, Minority Leader of the House of Representatives

"Mr. Curtis's method of managing weaves a path for effectively accomplishing the mission of the organization through firm but compassionate leadership. Leaving trendy management theories behind, he offers straightforward and practical applications for developing human resources to a higher level of competency and accountability, while dramatically increasing client/customer relations. Both proactive and logical, implementing these approaches would benefit both new and seasoned managers."
Wendy J. Keating, Commissioner of Labor, State of Montana, Retired

"The years I spent working with and being supervised by T. Gary Curtis were among the most challenging for me as a manager. Gary's mentoring and coaching style encouraged and empowered me to be a much better supervisor. I was not only a better manager, I was a much happier and healthier person when we parted ways after working together to manage a couple of very complex human service programs."
Candi Standall, Weatherization Program Director, Rocky Mountain Development Council, Retired

"I originally hired Gary Curtis as an administrator and then proudly watched as his management style challenged employees to improve so that they could move on to other management positions. Three different governors appointed three managers who worked for Gary to cabinet level positions in Montana state government."
David E. Fuller, Retired Commissioner of Labor, Lewis and Clark County Commissioner, and State Senator

"No other manager, leader, or mentor had more impact on my career than T. Gary Curtis. Gary was a visionary who nurtured my leadership abilities and taught me to cultivate my own vision, which triggered my career to propel in an upward spiral. I connected to his coaching and endeavored to develop the talent to manage in a similar way. I had a successful career as a leader because of his focus on staff development."
Lynn Long, former Bureau Chief, Montana State Personnel Division

"I have learned so many things from Gary. He is a born leader with the ability to transfer the skills needed to be a leader to other persons. Using skills Gary taught or demonstrated, I gained three different bureau chief positions over time, each with more responsibility and higher grade levels. Eventually, I became a division administrator. I believe anyone can benefit from reading this publication."
Dennis Zeiler, Administrator, Unemployment Insurance Division, Retired

"Gary teaches time-tested techniques to promote strong leadership and management of people and organizations. The participatory nature of Gary's management techniques generate staff buy-in and peer support—a very good basis of sound, easy to use, principles for the new supervisor or experienced administrator."
Karlene Grossberg, Bureau Chief, Montana Department of Public Health and Human Services, Retired

"Gary gave me assignments, the training and the tools needed to do the job, and specific due dates for completion. He also provided staff an opportunity to solve any problems that might arise on their own before coming to him. Staff and management seemed to function well within this management approach. I used the same style of management during my time as a bureau chief."
Mark Bowlds, Bureau Chief, Workforce Service Division, Retired

"Right after Gary became our administrator, I went into his office and asked him how he wanted me to handle a situation. He asked me how I thought it should be handled. I was astounded because we had never before been encouraged to voice an opinion. I learned from him that asking people what they think is the best way to help people learn how to think. It was a lesson I took with me in every management position I had."
Marla Hagen, Local Office Manager

Dedication

This book is dedicated to my family: my wife, Helen Curtis; our three children and their spouses, Melissa Romano, Jennifer and Kelly Williams, and Geoff and Andrea Curtis; and perhaps most of all to our six grandchildren: Brody, Aila, Mason, Aneea, Samantha, and Grant.

I hope this book gives my grandchildren a sense of my values and personality they can hold onto throughout their lives.

4 ever and 4 always; I love you dearly,

PAPA

Acknowledgments

In addition to my family, I'd like to acknowledge the friends who have made this book possible. Jerry Craig donated many hours of his time, edited the initial manuscript and asked good questions, which kept the book targeted to its intended audience. Bruce Midgett helped format the original manuscript and provided encouragement. Without their help and encouragement, this book would not have been written.

And, of course, I'm indebted to the professionals who helped me learn management and became good friends in the process. Dave Fuller set a standard for excellence; Laurie Ekanger taught me about the need for structure in office communications; and Mark Bowlds practiced delegation in a way that ensured our goals were met; Gregg Groepper showed me the value of work planning. They have been great role models for me in developing leadership and management skills.

Georganne O'Connor, owner of *Bright Ideas*, a book development company, is another longtime friend. Georganne did the final edit and performed all the professional work needed to get this book ready for publication. She was particularly helpful with organizing the material in the book. Without her, the book would not have been published.

Several other friends also read the manuscript in its various drafts and provided valuable thoughts on editing or content. All these friendships, which started between the mid-1960s and the mid-1970s have been important in my life.

I'm thankful for these friends and their support.

Contents

Preface

The following chapters present a personal hands-on story of my growth over more than 30 years as a supervisor and division administrator for the State of Montana and with private nonprofit organizations. In that time, I was fortunate to mentor supervisors and provide advice for numerous management problems. Each problem helped me develop insights about how supervisors can make a positive difference, not only to the quality of products and services but to staff development.

Over time, I have become convinced that a supervisor of any work unit can start a process I call "the upward spiral" to create a working environment or workplace culture that fosters continuous improvement.

I use the term upward spiral because twice I was assigned to supervise organizations I believed were in a downward spiral. Employees suffered from bad morale, little staff development existed, budgets were mismanaged, and timelines were ignored or became frantic last-minute emergencies. In response to these situations, we had to change business practices, reorganize work units, and remove some employees. However, none of these actions would have changed the workplace culture without the long-term management practices described in this book.

Using these management practices resulted in continuous improvement in work processes, work products, and, maybe most importantly, employees' skills and their abilities to work more independently. The organizations were able to weather the inevitable disruptions as a result of changes in personnel, budgets, products, legislation, and other distractions. And, in spite of these challenges, the organizations managed their budgets, met their timelines, and produced quality work while providing good customer service.

This primer describes the kinds of management structures and management behaviors it takes to start the work unit toward the upward spiral and continuous improvement. Perhaps, in my experience, the most pertinent part of the upward spiral has been observing changes in a workplace when staff were allowed to develop skills to operate more independently, which allowed managers to concentrate more on leading an organization and less on daily supervisory decisions. As staff did their jobs more efficiently, and supervisors used their time more effectively, the upward spiral had begun.

This book is based on some material I developed for a new supervisor's class at a "free university" in downtown Helena and additional information created for a delegation class I presented as a part of the Montana Professional Development Center's Essentials of Management training series.

Most information provided in the following chapters is based on mistakes: those I made and those I watched others make as well as lessons learned as a result. In addition, the chapters provide insights gained from watching good supervisors and from achieving positive results myself.

CHAPTER 1
THE SUPERVISOR'S INFLUENCE

All supervisors need to be a boss, manager, and leader.

The threat of being laid off as a division administrator for the State of Montana made me stop and study how I did my job. I believed my 30-person division would be consolidated, almost without notice, into a 350-person division with a similar purpose, and I would be out of a job.

At the time, I wanted to understand what our division had done that made it seem like such a good place to work and how to replicate the work environment and productivity, if I ended up with another management job. So I agreed to present management training because I knew preparing for each class would force me to think clearly about what management's role had been in building the environment and productivity.

This chapter provides some basic principles I've learned that helped me make a positive difference in my work as a supervisor. Using these principles can lead not only to increasing the quality of products and services, but improving staff development and the workplace culture.

What Difference Should a Supervisor Make?

In preparing the training, the first thing I tried to do was define, in simple terms, a supervisor's essential responsibilities and what difference a supervisor should make. Because I was looking for a concise description, I noted just a few responsibilities: policy, planning, delegating, evaluating, and administrative support. I thought it was a fairly good list, but something was missing. The next day, I decided I needed to better define supervision, so I added:

- Policy - What you want to do
- Planning - How to get it done
- Delegation – Doing it
- Evaluation - Continuous improvement
- Administrative Support – Maintaining it.

But I still felt like something was missing. So the next day, I showed these definitions to another manager and explained what I was trying to do. She looked at the list for just a few seconds before she said, "I'm sure what's bothering you is that you don't do any of these things." Her comment surprised me, and even seemed rude, but then she said, "What you do is require that we set up and maintain the systems that ensure these things get done and are done well." Finally, it made sense.

Take charge of your job—Don't let it be in charge of you

Although it took another manager to help me realize this truth, I now know the first step in taking charge of a management job is to realize your primary role is to organize and supervise the work, not do the work. So many people get caught in this basic mistake that it's worth emphasizing the point.

Don't do the work

Many supervisors are promoted to their positions because they are good at performing the job responsibilities. Often they are promoted without being provided any training on how to be a supervisor. They're just expected to know how. All of this makes new supervisors inclined to settle into tasks they're familiar with, the ones that got them promoted, so they end up doing the job instead of supervising the job. Although it's true that a few virtuoso pianists can play beautifully at a young age, few people are virtuoso managers or find that the job comes naturally. For most people, supervising is a learned skill you have to study and practice just like the piano.

Maintain a sense of urgency—Absolutely avoid a sense of panic

In the old days, door-to-door vacuum cleaner and encyclopedia salesmen made their living off of decisions their customers made under pressure. (Many car dealerships still try to use this pressure technique.) I believe most people who bought those items were young and inexperienced couples, who then spent the next twenty-four months making monthly payments that they resented and often could not really afford. Good decisions are made overnight; bad decisions are made under pressure.

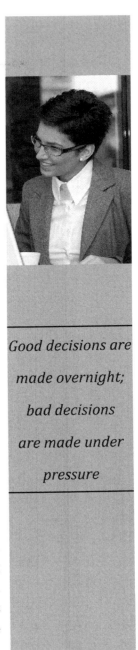

Good decisions are made overnight; bad decisions are made under pressure

Be a boss, manager, and leader

All supervisors need to be a boss, a manager, and a leader. Each of these words is meant to describe a different role you must play if you're going to fulfill all your job responsibilities. See Table 1.

In the "boss" role, you must make short-term and generally directive decisions. In the "manager" role, you have to ensure management systems, including a structure for ensuring staff development, are set up and maintained. In the "leader" role, you act as a visionary, looking to the future to anticipate and solve problems. As a leader, you also have to set quality standards and lead the work unit in its effort to achieve continuous improvement.

Don't get stuck in one role

As a supervisor, you need to recognize that if you want to help your work unit run more smoothly, become more productive, and benefit from better morale, you have to find a way to balance your time among all three roles. Generally, as the number of people you supervise or the complexity of the work increases, it's appropriate to shift time away from the boss role toward the leader role. I want to emphasize that all supervisors need to spend time in all three roles.

When called into a workplace to mentor a supervisor, I often find the person's main problem is that they're stuck in one role, frequently it's the boss role. Supervisors often let themselves get so overwhelmed with reacting to what seems like the daily or hourly crisis that they never get control of their jobs. But you must understand it's not enough, or even appropriate, to spend a lot of time reacting to a situation. If you spend too much time reacting, you'll constantly be under pressure and won't have enough time to make the best decisions.

Table 1. THE RESPONSIBILITIES OF A SUPERVISOR

AS A BOSS	AS A MANAGER	AS A LEADER
Daily decisions/ This week	*A month/A year*	*This year/Future*
Jane is sick, Bill will cover	Setting up management systems	Mission
The due date is	Evaluations systems	Goals
The boss wants	Work plans	Legislation
Maintenance	Distributing work	Continuous improvement
	Approving vacation schedules	Innovation
	Establishing budgets	Performance quality
	Job descriptions/ Staff development	Customer service
	Policy	
	Succession	

The decisions you make under pressure frequently fail, or partially fail, and cause you to react again. This adds to your workload, because you have to re-evaluate decisions or redo work on a project you've already implemented. This time-consuming process creates the perception of a crisis situation, which increases the probability you'll make another hasty and poor decision. The effort required to correct errors is called rework and often is even more expensive and unproductive than dealing with personnel grievances.

If you get stuck in the manager role, you'll likely face problems of a more-immediate nature. For example, customer service probably won't receive adequate attention, and no one will be anticipating future problems. If you get stuck in the leader role, you might present a lot of ideas and maybe begin a lot of projects, but the projects won't be completed.

Balance all three roles

Sometimes a new supervisor is more of a lead worker than a full-time supervisor. Their assignment might be to supervise less experienced or less successful workers while doing the same work their employees do.

For example, a three-person sales unit is responsible for forty accounts, and each sales associate is assigned fifteen accounts, which leaves ten accounts for the supervisor to handle in addition to being the supervisor (lead worker). In this case, the supervisor is responsible for doing the same work as the other employees, but must also make sure management systems are in place to ensure the work gets done well and on time. A lead worker probably spends most supervisory time in the boss role, but still needs to spend some time as a manager and a small amount of time as a leader. Even a person in a junior management position needs to understand they cannot provide the support senior management needs and expects if time and effort are not spent on "leader" issues.

However, the head of a large, complex workplace needs to spend most supervisory time in the leadership role, and hopefully, little time in the boss role because they have an experienced and competent staff. Occasionally, though, almost every employee will need clear short-term direction or redirection. So, even a governor or major corporate president has to be willing to step into the boss role once in a while if they're going to give senior managers the firm direction they need and expect.

Share Responsibility and Decision Making with Staff

At some point as a supervisor, you'll have to decide how much you want to share decision-making authority and responsibility with your staff. Making decisions in a work unit can be as simple as "the boss decides" or as complex as holding a staff vote. Table 2 shows a continuum of possible levels of employee involvement in decision-making based on five different management styles ranging from authoritarian to democratic:

- Directive
- Consultative
- Participatory
- Consensus
- Democratic.

As a supervisor, my goal was always to develop the skills of my staff to the point we could operate within a consensus decision-making process. A few management teams I worked with developed those skills and maintained them for at least short periods of time, but it

Table 2. MANAGEMENT STYLES

DIRECTIVE	CONSULTIVE	PARTICIPATORY	CONSENSUS	DEMOCRATIC
The Supervisor	*The Supervisor*	*The Supervisor*	*Supervisor & Team*	*Team has joint authority*
	Asks for input	Asks for input		
Makes decisions	Makes decisions	Sets direction	Sets direction jointly by vote	Sets direction
Tells people what to do	Explains how or why	*The Team* Discusses ideas, problems, solutions		
Takes total responsibility	Takes responsibility	Takes joint responsibility	Have joint responsibility	Has joint responsibility

BOSS
Supervisors operating in the boss role will tend to work on the left side of this chart.

MANAGER
Supervisors operating in the manager role will tend to work in the center of this chart.

LEADER
Supervisors operating in the leader role will tend to work on the right side of this chart.

was always an ongoing effort. Consensus management was a goal to work toward, not a destination I expected to arrive at quickly or operate with for long. That's because it's difficult to maintain the right balance of constructive disagreement and teamwork for long periods. This is partly due to the inevitable staff turnover, but also, as a management team gets more comfortable with each other, members tend to become more reluctant to challenge each other. It's hard to keep the right levels of trust and acceptance in balance without a willingness to challenge and disagree with each other.

As you allow staff more involvement in decision-making, you also provide more opportunity for staff development and a greater likelihood that employees will accept personal responsibility for the results of the decision.

Directive management

Directive management is authoritarian. Supervisors using this style present policy or procedure changes as *fait accompli*. They don't provide an opportunity for workers to comment, and generally do not want any comments. The supervisor simply implements the desired change by announcement or written memo.

Directive management probably is most appropriate with inexperienced staff and in agencies and businesses that need high security because of vulnerability to fraud and high turnover. Some say this management style causes high turnover. But some businesses, such as those around college campuses, may need directive management because the labor pool is inexperienced, and there's high turnover because employees are so mobile.

But, remember, if you operate primarily in this management mode, you'll spend most of your time in the boss role, which is primarily reactive. And, because this style stifles staff initiative and inhibits staff development, you'll probably have difficulty taking charge of your job unless you employ a small number of workers who perform similar, low-skilled jobs.

Consultative management

Consultative management is probably best described as a process for allowing workers to comment when policies or procedures are changed. Some employees cynically describe it as a style used by supervisors who pretend to want to hear their ideas but aren't willing to listen.

Participatory management allows staff to "have their say, if not their way"

This decision-making style doesn't authorize staff to make changes or influence management decisions. Supervisors may or may not consider staff comments, and usually, they make little effort to use consultation to encourage employees to assume personal responsibility for their work. Often when employees believe they have influenced a decision that affects them, they will buy in to the decision and work to make it succeed.

If you operate primarily in this management mode, you'll need to take most of the initiative and make most of even the smallest decisions. Again, as with directive management, you'll have difficulty taking charge of your job unless you have a small number of employees who perform similar, low-skilled jobs.

Participatory management

Participatory management allows staff to "have their say, if not their way." It's designed to ensure a supervisor listens to and heeds staff suggestions. It's not unusual, though, for staff members who comment in writing, but don't discuss comments and alternatives with management, to feel as if they have not been heard.

At one point while supervising a number of remote sites across the state, I started to hear employees complain about not being heard. I realized that, frequently, when the management team asked for input on an issue, such as providing directions, about one third of the sites said go "south," one third said they didn't care, and the other third said go "north," absolutely go "north." When the management team considered this advice, they concluded staff in the remote sites should have the flexibility to make their own decision on this issue and choose for themselves whether to go north or south.

Of course, this decision gave anyone inclined to complain the opportunity to legitimately say the decision didn't meet their needs, because the management team didn't impose their specific recommendations on all sites. Staff from some sites complained because they wanted management to tell everyone they had to go "north" or "south." Another site complained because they didn't want to take responsibility for deciding, they just wanted someone to tell them what to do.

Each work unit thought every work unit should do things the same way—the way they did it! I certainly believe in consistency in computer systems, inventory systems, and financial systems, but consistency in areas such as what constitutes quality customer service can have different meanings in different locations.

One main goal of participatory management is to encourage staff members to take more personal responsibility for their jobs by allowing them more influence over the policies that affect their jobs. Participatory management helps discourage "upward delegation," because you can require staff members to bring suggested solutions to the table when they bring a problem. This pushes staff to take initiative and helps you with decision-making, which usually results in better decisions and more staff commitment to make the policies work. Consequently, there's less rework, and you have more time to spend on other important projects. The upward spiral of staff development and improved work products can begin.

Consensus management
One theory of consensus management says everyone on the decision-making team has to agree with the decision about a new direction, policy, or change in procedure. This can be difficult if you have several strong personalities in the room, each with their own set of values and, perhaps, agendas based on their responsibility to represent different work units.

So, you often have to accept decisions all employees don't completely agree with but no one strongly objects to. And, to move forward with dramatic changes, you may have to accept decisions that concern some members of the decision-making team very much. Although managing by consensus as a means of ensuring thorough discussions is a good objective, it would be foolhardy to insist on it for every decision. Normally little would be accomplished, or the decision-making team wouldn't provide much constructive criticism or original thinking.

I can't imagine being able to consistent-ly get a consensus from a group of more than three team members when the decision would result in significant change or require a significant investment in an un-proven innovation. So, although it's good to place high value on working constructively together, it's probably not constructive to insist on consensus for every decision.

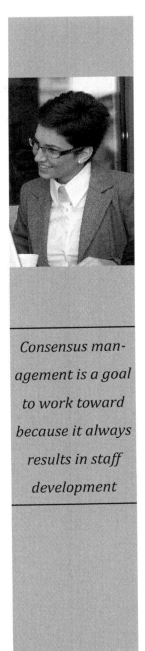

Once the team has reached a consensus, they're committed to support the decision. It's inappropriate to criticize the outcome to other staff members and certainly not to customers, especially if they haven't made it clear they can't support the decision. After one consensus management decision-making meeting, I heard a team member say, "They are making me do this." As the employee's supervisor, I reminded him immediately that he was part of "they," and I expected him to support the team's decisions, particularly if he had not made an effort to present better options himself.

Consensus management is a goal to work toward because it always results in staff development

I've found that moving toward consensus management is valuable because the effort pushes all team members to develop, accept personal responsibility, and carry an equal share of the responsibility and authority. This allows the team to make better decisions and use their time more efficiently, which results in better productivity and higher morale. When this is true, the upward spiral will start to take effect, and continuous improvement will occur.

Democratic management

Democratic management would require all employees to vote on policy changes. In my experience, the only work units I can imagine using this process would be professional partnerships of attorneys, accountants, or doctors. Maybe a rock band could use it. I know some businesses operate as co-operatives where all employees vote on everything of consequence, but I have no experience with that kind of organization. In my experience, about the only time democratic management would be appropriate would be if you were voting on where to hold the office picnic.

CHAPTER 2
LEADERSHIP

*Successful leaders leave a legacy of committed,
competent employees who understand how to provide
outstanding performance, strong customer service,
and continuous innovation and improvement.*

I have worked for good leaders and have tried to be a good leader. I've also read definitions of leadership that inspired me; however, most definitions described leadership in very specific ways, such as leadership in innovation. To me, a leader is someone with the ability not only to motivate and inspire people, but with the foresight and skills to create new leaders. I've concluded that the best evidence of outstanding leadership is a workplace that has been transformed in a positive way and is sure to continue to improve once the current leader is gone.

Successful leaders leave a legacy of committed, competent employees who understand how to provide outstanding performance, strong customer service, and continuous innovation and improvement. As a supervisor, you can work hard and put in long hours, but no supervisor lasts forever. That's why I've become such a strong advocate for all supervisors to take responsibility for staff development. When they leave a work unit, leaders need to hand over ingrained management systems and employees who understand the value of those management systems so the workplace transformation won't be lost.

One of the most satisfying aspects of my job as a supervisor has been observing changes in workplaces where staff were allowed to develop skills to operate more independently. This allowed supervisors to concentrate more on leading the organization and less on daily supervisory decisions. As staff did their jobs more efficiently, and the supervisors used their time more effectively, the upward spiral began.

Good Leaders

A good leader focuses on making a long-term difference, not only to the quality of an organization's products and services but to the development of staff and the workplace culture as a whole. In my experience, following the few simple practices presented below can help engage staff and promote productivity.

Promote positive attitudes

Employee attitudes present a major challenge for supervisors. Positive and negative attitudes can significantly affect staff performance and customer service. We know employees are much more productive if they have a positive attitude toward their work and feel connected and committed to the overall success of the organization. We also know how staff with negative attitudes can decrease trust and productivity.

Supervisors who are good leaders set up systems that encourage staff to buy into the organization's work processes and take personal responsibility for their work. They build a positive attitude by helping staff understand why their jobs make a difference to the success of the organization.

Some years ago I watched a film, which unfortunately I can't now give specific credit to, where the speaker said it's important for supervisors to give staff information about the "why" of a job, instead of just the "what." If I remember correctly, the speaker went on to say that good supervisors explained the "what and the why," and then they got out of the way for the "how."

To me, this means you share as much information as possible about what the job is, why it's important, and what performance standards you expect. But give employees as much leeway as possible to bring their own skills, abilities, and personalities to accomplish the job.

Good employees thrive in a system that persuasively describes the value of the work, allows good information exchange, and permits them to take personal responsibility for their work. This process helps them grow professionally.

Help staff commit to outstanding work performance

Strong leaders show a commitment to outstanding work performance in terms of quality, quantity, and timeliness of work. As a supervisor, employees often challenged me when I said I wanted quality

Strong leaders show a commitment to outstanding work performance in terms of quality, quantity, and timeliness

and quantity, saying I couldn't have both. But I always challenged them to reach for the largest amount of work they could produce in a quality fashion.

I've encountered a dichotomy of attitudes in employees. On the one hand, if staff didn't buy into the value of a project goal, they often resisted it, and said it couldn't be accomplished.

On the other hand, staff who accepted the goal and found enthusiasm for its value and purpose, often underestimated the amount of effort they needed to accomplish the goal. They committed to producing more work under shorter deadlines than they reasonably could accomplish. An outstanding leader helps staff build commitment to doing the job well and then lets their enthusiasm determine the quantity.

Challenge staff to think about better ways of doing business

All employees need to understand that change is inevitable and is almost always good. Good leadership requires supervisors to challenge staff to think about better ways of doing business and understand why innovation is important to them as employees and to customers. Leaders demonstrate an interest and a willingness to hear staff suggestions for improving products, services, and how customers are treated.

So if you want to be a leader, particularly if you want to leave a legacy, work on staff development. Build morale through employee attitude, improve performance through good communication and training, and improve products and services through continuous improvement.

Supervisory Styles

I suspect if we did a scientific study, we'd find that more extroverts move toward management positions than introverts do. It's probably just more natural for extroverts to assert themselves in leadership positions. That doesn't mean I think extroverts find it easier to be effective, or even that their outgoing nature makes it easier for them to be popular.

I do believe it's important to understand your natural supervisory style, its strengths and weaknesses, and build management systems and staff to complement them. If you're an introvert, you may wish to meet with people more one on one and hire someone to present training sessions for you. If you're an extrovert, you may choose to present the training yourself and meet with larger groups. Either can work, as long as you set up the proper systems to ensure good communication and staff involvement.

As an extrovert, I seemed to feel the need to get out and walk around to talk with staff. But one manager I respected the most almost always sat behind her desk. I made people feel special by going out to see them. She made people feel special by giving them private one-on-one attention when they needed her help. Her less gregarious style was just as effective and maybe more efficient.

Act consistently—Be positive

Good leaders act consistently and bring a positive attitude to work. One of the most demoralizing traits a supervisor can have is inconsistency. It doesn't matter if the inconsistency is a result of a personality trait, such as being controlling or moody, or arbitrary in decision making.

If you bring moodiness to the workplace, you put your staff in the position of guessing which days are good to approach you and which are not. Obviously, this is not a productive use of time, and eventually discourages employees from making suggestions or requests.

If you have problems at home, leave them there. The people you supervise aren't paid to put up with your inability to control your emotions. But, this doesn't mean I believe you should pretend to be happy when you're not or otherwise hold your emotions inside.

Once I witnessed a supervisor who withheld his disapproval of staff members until he blew up. Frequently, he'd approach the staff member the next day to overcompensate for his anger in some inappropriate way. As a supervisor, you have to find a way to deal with life's setbacks without allowing them to cause you to send mercurial messages at work. For example, don't send a staff member a message delegating responsibility and authority on a day you feel good and then try to control the project just because you're in a bad mood. My point is that, as a supervisor, you get paid to lead, and to lead well you need to be positive about the work and you need to be consistent. You should display a good attitude and good morale, not be the cause of frustrations and low morale.

Take advantage of diversity to complement your skills

Everyone brings their personality to work. To do the best job you need to understand your strengths and weaknesses. I've found it's often helpful to purposely hire people who complement your strengths. If you're a natural visionary but weak on follow through, it's obviously important for you to discipline yourself to lay out a plan and stick to it. But it may make the job a lot easier if you have a 'partner' who is naturally detail and process oriented.

Early in my time as a supervisor, I thought I had the right instincts for delegating and building trust relationships one on one. However, I had almost no experience and no particular insight into setting up and maintaining professional management systems such as staff meetings to share information efficiently with an entire staff. Luckily, I hired as my second-in-command a professional named Laurie who did. Laurie immediately set out to develop better communication, better work planning, and better filing systems.

When Laurie was promoted and left our work unit, I told her I believed I could have made sure employees were treated fairly and probably maintained a workplace with generally good morale, but without her help I couldn't have created such a professional and productive workplace. Her abilities complemented my strengths, and in the process of setting up systems, she taught me some needed skills and made me a better supervisor, which meant I received more respect from my superiors.

Because of this respect, it wasn't long before my superiors increased my responsibilities, which required me to concentrate more on leadership issues than I had previously.

In one situation, I was pushed into a work unit that needed a better culture of customer service and a visionary who could promote changes in business practices that would keep the unit current with technology. Again, I was lucky to have my skills balanced by a partner, Mark, who had a natural talent for management. Mark placed high value on fairness, timeliness, and follow through, and he liked to joke he was lazy enough to be excellent at delegation.

In that case, I'd envision the needed change and work to get staff to accept the change, and Mark would make sure we were consistent

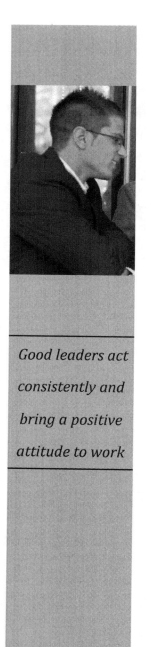

Good leaders act consistently and bring a positive attitude to work

and followed through on previous changes we had implemented. Once again I had a great partner. The point is that because I hired management partners who had different skills than I did, I became a better supervisor.

Many people try to avoid conflict by hiring people who are similar to them. I've even witnessed workplaces where supervisors expected staff to emulate their wardrobes if they wanted to be promoted. Apparently, those supervisors weren't secure enough to have all that second-guessing and those different opinions around. If I'd had those fears, I would have been much less successful as a manager and leader, because my ability would not have been complemented nearly as well.

Once I led a management team with whom I was very comfortable because we seemed to have a high degree of unanimity. Decisions and projects always seemed to flow easily, especially at the beginning of each project. Then one day I showed up for a meeting with a legal pad full of notes. I looked across my notes at the management team and said, "I think we have a problem with intake and wonder if you have any ideas for what we should do about it?" Mark leaned toward me and asked, "What do you have written down on that paper? If you already know what you want us to do why don't you just tell us so we can get after it?" At that point, I realized the reason the team seemed to work so well together was that the other members had just been agreeing with whatever I said.

It certainly felt like a compliment to me that we had experienced enough success for the management team to trust my leadership, but the result was other team members weren't voicing their criticism of what I proposed. As a result, it wasn't unusual for unforeseen problems to show up after we had implemented a project.

Mark's comment at the meeting seemed like a warning that the rest of the management team wanted to be more involved in decision making. We no longer had six brains working toward consensus on the best decision, direction, and work plan; we had five brains reinforcing one brain. Because we weren't doing enough critical thinking, we didn't always anticipate problems.

On a really good management team, people feel comfortable disagreeing, and luckily, Mark felt comfortable enough to challenge me. But each team member is responsible for fulfilling their role, even if their ideas conflict with another member's role. A team is made stronger when everyone performs their individual responsibility to voice opinions, especially in their area of expertise, not by just getting along, or even worse, following along. There is enormous value in constructive disagreement.

As a result, we made three changes to our management team meetings to ensure we shared and benefited from our different perspectives and experiences, instead of just reinforcing each other. First, we talked about teamwork and discussed decisions that could have made better if team members had challenged me and each other more. Second, we made sure that, from then on, we rotated the role of meeting facilitator among all team members. Third, we agreed each facilitator should spend a few minutes going around the table to make sure every team member had a chance to speak and be heard on all topics before we made a decision.

Also, I made it a point not to speak up as often as I had, and definitely not early in the discussion, except to ask questions. I reserved my input until the rest of the group had discussed the subject long enough to find some significant point of disagreement or consensus. Asking questions instead of stating opinions, and listening to the interactive discussion, helped me better evaluate problems and receive the best advice from the management team.

CHAPTER 3
THE STRUCTURE WILL SET YOU FREE

Structure—work plans, job descriptions, goals, consistent written policies and procedures, and regular staff communications—can turn a downward spiral into an upward spiral.

The purpose of this book is to help you become an effective manager, someone who can create a work environment that fosters productivity, staff development, and good morale. Structure is the key to making this happen.

Most managers spend too much time reacting to "emergencies," which lets their jobs take charge of them. But if you set up and maintain management systems that provide structure, you can take charge of your job. As many managers will attest, if you continually work in crisis mode, eventually your work group will spiral downward, which diminishes productivity, increases staff frustrations with management, and increases turnover.

Structure can turn a downward spiral into an upward spiral. For our discussion, structure means project planning; consistent written policies and procedures, including hiring and promotion guidelines; and structured staff communication.

The Value of Job Descriptions, Work Plans, and Goals

A senior manager once told me that most new supervisors don't really gain the respect of their staff and take charge of their work units until they reorganize and change people's job duties or fire someone. Generally, that might be true. But I believe a better approach is to significantly influence the workplace culture by establishing a set of values for the unit's direction and productivity.

The most constructive way to do this is to set clear, high standards for work performance and customer service. Developing written job descriptions, work plans, and goals are an important step in accomplishing this and helping take charge of your work unit. They minimize your day-to-day guidance of staff and allow you more time to manage and lead. This presents the opportunity for you to start the upward spiral.

Job descriptions

Most people want to work, and they want to make a difference when they're at work, so job descriptions are essential to their productivity. They are also your first step in delegating and assigning primary job responsibilities. For most jobs, it would not be reasonable or fair to ask employees to operate without a written description of their roles and responsibilities.

Work plans

A work plan provides a structured approach for outlining project goals and the approaches needed to accomplish the goals. It breaks down work processes into achievable tasks and identifies what you want to accomplish and who will make this happen.

A work plan is really a job description for the work unit. It illustrates each person's responsibilities and shows how they complement the rest of the team's efforts. As such, work plans provide a primary way to build teamwork. I find teamwork is often more about each employee taking care of their personal responsibilities for the good of the team, than it is about doing things together or even doing the same things.

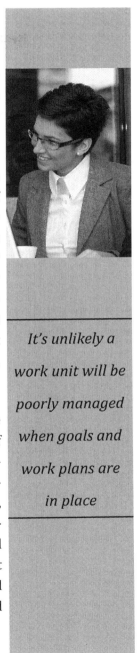

Still, you can't build a team if you develop a work plan and don't share it with all staff responsible for doing the work. I've frequently encountered supervisors who have developed work plans that included their expectations of staff, and maybe even their managers' expectations, but the responsible employees didn't know the expectations even existed. As a supervisor, you should not only share work plans with your employees, but involve them in developing the plans.

It's unlikely a work unit will be poorly managed when goals and work plans are in place

I'm not saying a work unit can't be productive without plans and goals. I have known lots of work units that operated productively without them. Usually, however, these organizations were small and staffed by experienced, self-driven people who communicated constructively. The larger work units grow and spread out (especially if some are located at remote sites), and the less experienced and motivated employees are, the more you need the structure work plans and goals provide.

It's not impossible to have a well-managed work unit without goals and work plans, but it is unlikely a work unit will be poorly managed when goals and work plans are in place. They are a very important step in your process to take charge of a work unit.

Goals and expectations

Clearly defined goals and expectations help staff focus on the most important work. Many employees fill their time with whatever part of their job they enjoy the most or what gives them the most reward. But, if you give staff a clear idea of what you expect of them and define the tasks most important to the work unit, those tasks will become the most important.

If employees are bored or unsure of what to do, they'll fill their time with something unimportant. They may be distracting other people from productive efforts, but it's just as likely they'll expand a small job to fill the time in some inefficient manner.

I once inherited a work unit where employees spent hours, month after month, calculating percentages by hand, when a computer could have done in minutes. There certainly was more productive work to be done, but because the supervisor hadn't identified staff goals or expectations, the employees didn't see the value of looking for a more efficient way of doing business. Filling time was their most important job responsibility. Because they hadn't been trained in current technology and hadn't taken the initiative to get training, they were prime candidates for layoffs.

Provide your staff with clearly written goals and expectations, so they're more likely to understand what work is most important to you and the work group, making those tasks the most important.

A Simple Planning Process

Providing structure to a work unit is little more than getting organized so the work can flow without getting mired in crisis and you can act rather than react to your job. Project planning provides the foundation for getting organized and creating other management systems. I've used the simple process shown here to help plan many projects and develop specific work plans to accomplish project goals. The most important thing to plan for is, of course, the accomplishment of job responsibilities.

Define your project

List every step or job responsibility you need to accomplish to ensure the project is done well, on time, and within budget constraints. Establish numerical or product goals for each job responsibility. For example, the project must meet federal performance standards, or the final product must weigh less than two pounds.

Determine who should do each task

Assign each job responsibility to the most appropriate employee. Assign responsibility for tasks according to the employee's area of work responsibility. If you assign several employees to accomplish a task, designate a leader and have them develop a work plan and schedule.

Determine how long the job will take and add 10%

Ask each employee or work unit to provide you with a reasonable estimate of time to complete their portion(s) of the project. For tasks of any size, add some small amount of time for unforeseeable holdups. And keep in mind most people will say they can accomplish a project far faster than is reasonably possible.

You do not have a policy if it is not in writing

Lay out your timeline and add a week

Bring all individual time estimates together to create a single timeline. Make sure each employee or work unit understands how their work fits into the overall project timeline. Establish interim measurement dates to review project status or draft proposals just to make sure you don't get to the end of some segment of the overall project and realize a staff member or work unit is not on track. For example, you might schedule a project review meeting every Monday morning.

If you have a project, such as a Request for Proposal, with a predetermined due date, start with the due date and work backward. This will help you make sure you actually have time to accomplish the task.

Plan to plan

Because most supervisors spend too much time reacting to their jobs instead of managing their work, it's important to take the initiative to manage your work by scheduling planning time well in advance. Most of us are too busy to develop a work plan this week, and in reality, probably too busy any time in the next two or three weeks. But if you look at your calendar and staff calendars for weeks farther out, schedules may be much more open. My point is you should not expect to do work planning immediately. You need to plan to plan. And give staff advance notice of the dates you want to reserve for planning, usually several weeks in advance. This is especially true if your employees haven't worked together on a planning effort before. And if you want to involve a large number of employees in the process, it's much more efficient to have a single staff person or small group develop and distribute a draft work plan for consideration by the larger group in advance of the meeting.

Written Policies and Procedures

A well-managed work unit also provides structure through written policies and procedures, usually distributed to employees as a handbook. Policies are principles or rules that guide consistent decision making and actions. They generally are based on federal, state, and local laws and play an important role in productivity.

Procedures establish an ordered set of tasks necessary to make decisions and perform actions based on the policies. They focus on the specific "who-does-what-when-and-where" elements of implementing a policy. Procedures might focus on guidelines and timelines for customer service and decision making, including how policies will be established and how budget decisions will be made. They also may cover employee time reporting, including who is eligible for overtime and when.

Put your policies in writing and operate within them consistently
I don't believe supervisors or work units can be successful without written policies and procedures and without operating within them consistently. In my career I worked for two supervisors who didn't put policies in writing, because they feared it would limit their management prerogatives. They wanted to maintain their ability to act arbitrarily.

I've found managers who act arbitrarily not only demoralize staff but invite staff grievances. Combating grievances ranks as one of a supervisor's most unproductive tasks and is often more expensive. Neither of my previous supervisors succeeded at their jobs because their continual arbitrary and inconsistent decisions led to problems, especially with personnel. These individuals ceased to be productive supervisors because they spent too much time dealing with disgruntled employees and their grievances rather than acting as a boss, manager, and leader.

Remember, independent arbitrators or mediators won't support a policy if it's not in writing or no evidence exists that the employees were aware of the policy. The lesson here is that, as a supervisor, "a policy" on any topic, must be in writing, circulated to staff members, and placed in office policy manuals. You do not have a policy if it is not in writing.

Develop a consistent interview process

Other important elements of an employee handbook are consistent policies detailing the work unit's hiring process, including how to conduct an interview. The interview process should include structured questions and answers that measure an applicant's ability to perform the job and thorough reference checks (this normally requires the applicant's permission) that measure an applicant's reliability and ability to work with others. Predetermined skills tests also are useful in measuring an applicant's ability to perform the job.

Many supervisors believe they are such good judges of character that they ask prospective employees in for an interview before they're prepared to measure the applicant's ability to do the job. Even if you think you already know someone well, your interview questions should measure skills the employee will need. For consistency, develop the questions in advance, based on the job description. You also should develop answers to the questions before the interview, so you'll be better able to measure the quality of an applicant's answer. If you're lucky, an applicant will provide an answer that is even better than the one you prepared, but generally this will not happen.

Then trust the interview process. If the process actually measures abilities to perform the job, the person who does best in the process should be hired. Let the process, not your personal bias, identify who should be hired.

Structured Communication

Every work unit needs consistent structured communication. As a supervisor, you're responsible for providing regular, accurate information to staff about everything that relates to their jobs, including hiring and promotion processes. But you'll never share enough information with staff if you don't also develop and maintain systems to distribute information through informational meetings, decision-making meetings, memos, and other forms of communication.

Share information to keep staff expectations in line with reality

During a time I call "the era of World War II management," supervisors frequently told employees they operated "on a need to know basis." If employees didn't need direct knowledge to perform their job, supervisors wouldn't share the information. This approach certainly had value for wartime industries and still is valuable for businesses trying to protect technological secrets related to software or drugs. It's even valuable for companies trying to control fraudulent claims by segregating parts of a claims process. Outside of these kinds of businesses, not sharing all the information just demoralizes the workforce.

In most workplaces today, you should provide employees with as much information as they need to bring forth their best initiative and suggestions for continuous improvement.

When you don't provide employees with good information about everything that relates to their jobs, including budgets, they don't take as much initiative and personal responsibility for their jobs, and they don't make good recommendations or independent decisions. If staff understand what you base your decisions on, they can participate in the decision-making process and make recommendations for improvement instead of feeling helpless or ignored.

Some kinds of information, such as new position announcements and opportunities for promotion, can greatly raise or lower staff morale. For example, if you have created an open and consistent process for hiring and promotions and shared it with all staff, you'll raise staff morale. If you don't openly share this process, staff members will usually believe you're manipulating it for the benefit of a particular person.

Sharing information about the stability of employment also is important. If rumors surface about potential layoffs and you don't provide as much truthful and candid information as possible, staff morale will plummet, and productivity will go down.

I also believe it's important for employees to have a reasonable understanding of budget limitations in their work units and how the budget affects their work so they know what is affordable in terms of equipment, training, or travel. Making this kind of information available to staff helps raise morale because people feel included and empowered. It also saves time because staff won't turn in equipment requests or travel requests that are unrealistic.

Hold regular information meetings

Again, you'll never share enough information with staff if you don't have several systematic ways to produce and distribute it. This includes scheduling information and coordination meetings where you notify staff in advance and distribute agendas before the meetings.

Most supervisors aim to conduct productive meetings where staff are well prepared and willing to share in the discussion. Scheduling meetings in advance and distributing an agenda before the meeting contribute to achieving this goal. When you give staff at least one day's notice, you'll increase your chances of all appropriate staff attending and using their work schedule more efficiently.

And sharing an agenda in advance gives staff time to think and prepare for the meeting. This increases the quality of discussion and, consequently, the quality of the meeting's result, another strong step toward the upward spiral.

You'll never share enough information with staff if you don't have several systematic ways of producing and distributing it

Also, keep a calendar of all meetings and topics. In addition to being a productive time management tool, keeping track of all meetings and topics discussed establishes a record for project planning and estimating time needed to complete a similar project. The record also becomes important in legal matters that might involve an employee grievance.

I admit, I often didn't look forward to these informational meetings. When I looked back at the work unit's accomplishments each year, however, I knew the regular information and coordination meetings were as helpful as any other management system I implemented.

Develop a process for making policy decisions
Distributing an agenda before a meeting is particularly helpful in meetings where policy decisions are made. But, it's more important to develop a process for meetings where you make decisions that affect the whole or large parts of the work group, and use it consistently. The process can be as simple as the one outlined below.

- A supervisor puts a policy item on the agenda, perhaps at the request of a staff member.

- Before the meeting, the supervisor ensures the policy item is distributed in writing for all staff to consider. The staff member who requested the policy, or a representative assigned by the supervisor, develops the first "discussion draft."

- Staff discuss the draft policy at a regularly scheduled meeting. The supervisor provides an opportunity for "affected staff," or their representative, to speak during the meeting.

- Staff either tentatively approve the policy as written, or return it to the author for specific revisions. In all cases, the policy will be included on the agenda for final discussion and a decision at the next scheduled meeting.

- During the next scheduled meeting, participants discuss the final policy and make a decision, again with the opportunity for affected staff or their representative to speak during the meeting. Staff should make an attempt to reach consensus; however, if that's not possible they should take a vote or the supervisor may need to decide. It's important for the supervisor to remain quiet during the discussion, except to ask questions or seek clarification until everyone has spoken. This increases staff involvement and doesn't stifle the discussion by stating an opinion too early in the process.

Once a decision has been made, support it and make every effort to live with it for at least several months. Many controversial decisions become "the way it always was," if they are kept in place for a few months. Using an approach like this assumes you are willing to allow staff members to participate in making policy decisions.

Signs of Good Management

Over many years of supervising staff and training supervisors, I've observed signs of good and poor management and how they impact staff. As Table 3 shows, signs of good management include written work plans, good information exchange, and written policies. Good management results in friendly, helpful staff, timely and error-free work, and staff initiative. On the other hand, poorly managed workplaces (Table 4) show signs of budget problems, frequently missed deadlines, and unbalanced workloads. In these work environments, staff absenteeism, turnover, and grievance rates are high while initiative and morale are low.

Table 3. SIGNS OF GOOD MANAGEMENT

Management Signs	Personnel Signs
• Written work plans, policies, and procedures	• Friendly, helpful staff
• Paper and electronic file systems	• High staff retention
• Good information exchange	• Timely work
• Structured, consistent hiring process	• Staff initiative
• Job descriptions and evaluations	• Constructive criticism of management
• Balanced staffing pattern	• Error-free work

Table 4. SIGNS OF POOR MANAGEMENT

Management Signs	Personnel Signs
• Budget problems	• High absenteeism
• Frequently missed deadlines	• High staff turnover
• Inconsistent policies	• High grievance rate
• Lost work/correspondence	• Low staff initiative
• Unbalanced workloads	• Severe criticism of management
• Inconsistent or arbitrary personnel decisions	• Poor morale

Most work groups will experience one or two of these poor management issues, or occasionally, several issues. Dealing with these recurring issues is a large part of why management is needed. To be effective, supervisors must address and resolve the issues before they affect the work unit. If you review the list of problems resulting from poor management and recognize several are prevalent in a work unit you supervise, it's time to look in the mirror to get a good view of these problems. Also, it's time for you to accept responsibility, as the supervisor: get help determining what is wrong, and learn how to do things differently.

The only time I ever went to a management training class the instructor asked each of us to tell him why we were there, or what we wanted out of the class. I happened to be the last person to speak, but I was the first person to say that I was there because I thought my management abilities were weak. Every other person in the room saw their problems as somebody else's shortcomings or failures. By the time the class was over, I thought most of them would have benefited from a long thoughtful look in the mirror.

CHAPTER 4
STAFF DEVELOPMENT

*The goal of the upward spiral is to create a workplace
where staff members become more independent
and supervisors spend more time actively managing and
leading instead of reacting. Staff development is your
most important long-term responsibility.*

As a supervisor, your most important short-range responsibility is, of course, to get the work done well and on time. Whether you're aiming to meet production goals, timelines, or service goals, the work has to come first. In the long run, however, staff development is the key to raising production goals, reducing timelines, and increasing service goals. If your goal is to begin the upward spiral, you have to have staff development.

Staff development means assisting staff acquire skills and knowledge for personal development and career advancement. It involves working with employees to change their knowledge, understanding, behaviors, and skills. Staff development also focuses on your management behaviors: how you communicate and interact with employees to create and nurture a positive workplace culture. In an upward spiral culture, supervisors recognize staff for their achievements, provide opportunities for them to think and act independently, and encourage them to take personal responsibility for their knowledge, skills, and behaviors.

Praise and Constructive Criticism

It's important for you to consistently recognize and reinforce your employees' hard work and achievements. Most employees want to believe their work is important. Some are happy to believe it's important because it pays well, but most want to feel like they're making a difference. It's also important to provide constructive feedback to staff on the strong and weak points of their performance.

Tell staff what they're doing right . . . early and often

Positive reinforcement is the most effective method of improving staff. My experience has shown that most staff members want to work, and not just because they want to have jobs and be paid. They want to be busy and productive while they're at work. So, if you provide clear guidance through written job descriptions, work plans, and goals, staff usually will work productively with little supervision.

When you provide positive reinforcement to staff, they happily continue in the direction they've been going. When they're on target, providing the productivity or quality of customer service you expect, reinforce their job-related behavior frequently. This will keep staff on task and make it easier for them to accept constructive criticism when necessary.

If employees don't feel appreciated, they're much more likely to try to gain attention and appreciation some other way, probably by doing work less connected to the unit's mission. When you don't provide constructive feedback or recognition, it's easy for staff to work on what they think is important (or enjoy) instead of what they were assigned. So, be aware and praise employees who are productive and provide the quality customer service you expect.

Never criticize an employee in public

To criticize an employee in front of their peers is one of the most demoralizing things you can do. I learned early in my life as a parent that if I criticized one child in front of another, I would encounter resistance, arguments, and anger. If I took the child away to a private room and started the conversation with "I love you," then explained why, because of my love, I couldn't allow their behavior to continue, I might hear a few excuses, but before long we would reach an agreement for better behavior and rejoin the family. My constructive criticism was accepted more readily because I avoided defensive reactions from my child.

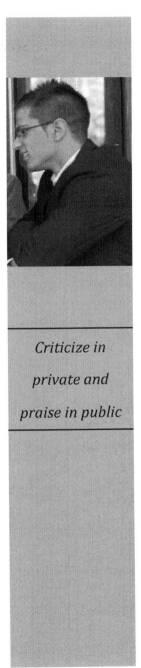

Criticize in private and praise in public

Sure, employees are adults and, as grown ups, theoretically more able to deal with criticism. But you'll still find that the rudeness of public criticism is hard for anyone to overlook. If you criticize employees in public, they're much more likely to become defensive and not even hear what you're saying. Instead of hearing what you actually say it's more likely employees will hear what they're afraid you'll say or wish you'd say. Remember, employees who become defensive are less able to concentrate and talk constructively about your concerns. Criticize in private and praise in public.

Do regular, job-related evaluations—Provide constructive criticism in every evaluation

Regularly scheduled performance evaluations are important to staff morale and the effectiveness of the workplace. In every evaluation you should provide constructive feedback on staff members' strengths and weaknesses. It's important you tell them what's right about their work so they know the value of their accomplishments and are encouraged to continue their performance. You also need to provide feedback on areas that need improvement; otherwise, people won't be likely to improve.

It's important for staff members to gain from your experience, insight, and judgment. If you don't help employees understand how to improve their performance, they'll usually continue to perform at the same or lower level. This is unfair to staff because they don't have the opportunity to grow and develop, and unfair to the work unit because its effectiveness or efficiency can't improve and, in other words, maintain an upward spiral.

Most people associate "criticism" with negative words or actions that put people down. But "constructive criticism," on the other hand, aims to build people up by identifying and finding solutions to problems in a positive way.

If, like many supervisors, you don't have the courage to face issues and provide constructive criticism on skills that need improvement, it will be much harder for staff to believe your positive feedback. If you only compliment employees without discussing areas they need to improve, you create a problem with trust. Staff may say, "I know there are some skills I need to work on but my supervisor didn't mention them. If I was not told the whole truth, how much truth was I told?"

To gain your staff's total respect, you have to tell them the total truth. Constructive criticism is the key. You want job evaluations to recognize and reward staff for what they do well in addition to helping them grow and have an honest chance at personal development.

Workplace Independence

The goal of the upward spiral is to create a workplace where staff members become more independent and supervisors spend more time actively managing and leading instead of reacting. In my experience, if you encourage employees to be independent at work, their skills and job satisfaction increase. And, as staff independence grows, you become more effective and efficient.

Avoid upward delegation

Requiring staff to do their own work and attempt to solve their own problems before they come to you is another practice that helps begin the upward spiral. I made a habit of immediately asking staff who came to me with a problem: "What do you recommend?" For follow-up questions, I usually fell back to: "What does the law say about this?" or "Do we already have related policy or procedures for this?" My questions were intended to encourage employees to use their own experience and abilities to solve a problem before bringing it to me.

If you follow the above practice, as employees get better at their jobs and act more independently, you can spend more time in the manager and leader roles instead of being bogged down reacting to day-to-day problems of the boss role. You can spend more time setting up and managing systems instead of dealing with each individual's crisis. It also means you'll have more time to think about and anticipate problems so the challenges can be met actively rather than reactively. You'll then become more effective and efficient, and staff will benefit from the results of better management. Soon rework will decrease, productivity will increase, and so will staff morale.

One day after I explained this practice to a group of intermediate supervisors, one said, "But if every time one of my staff members brings a problem to me, and I ask them what they recommend, they will quit bringing problems to me."

I just stood there quietly, but a few people in the room chuckled, and that supervisor soon realized most of us thought it would be good for employees to solve more of their own problems.

If you don't set out to delegate everything, you'll never delegate enough

Delegate everything—If you don't delegate something because you think you can do it better, you're probably too insecure or too arrogant to supervise

Supervision requires trust. If you don't trust people to make their own decisions, they can never learn, grow, and accept more personal responsibility. As a result, you can't start the upward spiral. Your employees won't have the opportunity to learn from their mistakes or successes and will never improve, and the work unit's productivity will decline instead of rise.

Delegate everything—If you think you can't delegate because it will take too long to teach your staff how to do a job, you're too selfish to be a supervisor

If you're too busy to take time to teach a staff member how to do a job, you just sentence yourself to being too busy the next time also. You won't get past reacting to emergencies and won't be able to move toward active management. Again, your employees won't develop and become more productive, morale will go down, and productivity will stagnate. Obviously, if you are a lead worker, you cannot delegate everything, and you shouldn't delegate job performance evaluations, but if you don't set out as a supervisor to delegate everything, you'll never delegate enough.

Keep the size of your staff slightly smaller than staff think is optimum—People perform better when they're busy

Note I said, "SLIGHTLY smaller" than your staff think is optimum. I recognize many businesses and government agencies budget fewer staff than the workload requires. I've experienced situations where a business or a legislature wanted to fund a token effort because there was some public relations benefit. I recognize these situations can frustrate and overwhelm supervisors and employees.

Still, almost everywhere I've worked or acted as a consultant, staff perceived more people were needed to do the job well. The irony is people seem to get along better, be more productive, and enjoy their jobs more when they are busy, not when they are overwhelmed.

You'll be better off as a supervisor having one less staff person than is optimum, than having one more. Of course, you want the optimum number of staff members, particularly if being short of staff will damage customer service or product sales. But people who are not busy tend to procrastinate more and find more to complain about, so be wary of requests for hiring more staff.

CHAPTER 5
RESOLVING PERSONNEL PROBLEMS

*The best approach for resolving personnel problems
is to identify and address issues quickly and consistently
and follow a constructive discipline process.*

All supervisors face personnel problems that can impact staff morale, performance, and productivity. In my experience, the best approach to resolving these problems is to identify and address issues quickly and consistently and follow a constructive discipline process. Constructive discipline is meant to motivate staff to improve their performance or behavior and prevent the problem from recurring.

Taking swift action is important in addressing a personnel problem. But, perhaps, the most important thing to remember about corrective discipline is that it's supposed to be constructive, and for that to happen you have discuss the issue with the staff member in a calm, non-threatening, and fair manner.

Problem Employees

Poor performance is a common personnel issue in many workplaces. For example, when supervising people in short-term or part-time jobs, I frequently dealt with attendance problems and even laziness. Frankly, in those situations, I found little value in going through a personnel process with repeated communications. Usually, I just terminated the employee and moved on.

In workplaces with more professional employees in more permanent jobs, I often found two different kinds of problems. One related to trouble with employees suffering from what I call "Excellence Syndrome." These staff members took their work too seriously, lost their sense of perspective, and became too defensive about change or criticism, although they worked hard. The other common problem in an established work force related to employees who had interpersonal relationship issues. Although these employees tended to be older, better educated, and better paid, they had poor social skills. Often these "problem employees" were productive enough and provided good-to-excellent customer service; however, their behavior just made work miserable for those around them. I've heard supervisors faced with similar issues say, "What can I do? They are good at their job." I always responded, "You and your other employees deserve a worker who is both productive and polite with customers, staff, and management."

Consequently, I want to emphasize that if you want a productive work group, you'll have to insist on staff members developing constructive personal relationships in addition to performing quality work. You may spend more time working on healthy relationships than on poor performance of job duties.

A problem employee now means there's a personnel problem— The same problem employee a year from now means there's a management problem

I frequently hear supervisors say, "You can't fire anyone anymore." And I say, "if you have a personnel problem now and you haven't resolved it within a year, you're most likely also a problem." Most of the time, you can resolve a problem within a few days. However, in some cases, it may take a year to reach resolution. For example, I have dealt with personnel problems, such as rudeness to coworkers or missed project deadlines where, after corrective action, the employee refrained from the offensive behavior for more than six weeks before it recurred. This consistent but infrequent occurrence of serious but not flagrant offenses caused the problem to drag on. If you will follow the advice provided in this chapter, and address issues quickly and consistently, personnel problems will be resolved within one year, and usually within three days.

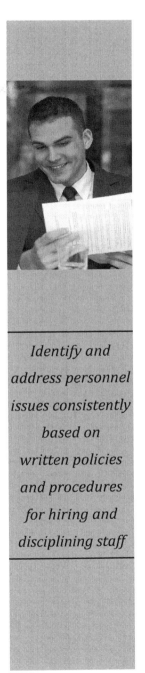

Identify and address personnel issues consistently based on written policies and procedures for hiring and disciplining staff

Rules for Discipline Problems—Do's

To create and maintain an upward spiral, you need to identify and address personnel issues consistently and persistently, based on written policies and procedures for hiring and firing staff. In most cases, you can resolve the problems quickly, especially when the staff member's offense isn't egregious and you have a constructive discipline policy in place or one exists as part of a bargaining agreement. The quicker you address a personnel issue, the quicker the problem will be resolved.

Constructive discipline polices differ among regions and organizations as they are based on company policy and state law. All state laws and or company policies may not require due process and just cause before an employee is terminat-

Typical Constructive Discipline Process
Step 1 - Informal interview
Step 2 - Formal corrective interview
Step 3 - Warning letter or suspension
Step 4 - Good faith and fair dealing letter of termination

ed. However, you want to be certain to follow state law, existing company policy, and/or union agreements to deal with personnel problems. You may not be required to provide a resolution process to deal with these problems. But if you do, at a minimum, use a process that includes these four steps: an informal interview, formal corrective interview, warning letter or suspension, and good faith and fair dealing letter of termination. When you do you'll help build morale, because your employees will believe there is a fair process for handling issues.

In my experience, most employees will correct their performance after step one, or they never will correct it. In a few cases, it may take up to a year to resolve a personnel issue. You may have to go through all four steps of the process, which means you'll have at least four difficult and time-consuming conversations with an employee before termination. However, even with the most onerous constructive disciplinary process, you can resolve personnel problems when you are consistent and persistent.

Say Four Things

During the first corrective disciplinary meeting, I tell staff four things:

1. What about their performance is a problem
2. Why it is a problem
3. What performance I expect instead
4. Why it is important.

This procedure, which I call the What/Why What/Why conversation is meant to be a formula to guide your discussion with any employee during an informal interview, step one of the process. I've probably used this formula in conversations with 150 staff members. Within three days of the conversation, approximately 130 of the employees corrected their performance or behavior. Only one of the other 20 employees ever improved. This meant that nothing in the corrective disciplinary process improved the employee's job performance if this first conversation did not. So, there's no point in procrastinating about taking step one, and even more importantly, there's no point in repeating a step in the process...just go the next step. I've found talking to the same employee repeatedly about the same or similar problems, without taking the next step, can be destructive to the disciplinary process.

I remember working with a supervisor who had raised concerns about an employee's tardiness ten times before he continued with the corrective disciplinary process. When the supervisor met with this employee and a union representative about a warning letter the supervisor had given the employee, the union representative asked, "How can you claim this is an important issue now after going a year without saying it was? What has changed in the last year to make this important?"

The union representative was comfortable the employee would win if the case went to arbitration. This was because the record showed the supervisor discussed the problem with the employee many times, but didn't take any action to hold the staff member accountable for not correcting the problem.

Luckily for the supervisor, the union representative knew the employee's tardiness was a problem for the staff member's coworkers (other union employees), so the union offered to negotiate a deal that would remove the letter from the employee's file in exchange for a fresh start and a commitment from the employee not to be late for work. By talking to the staff member about tardiness over and over without holding him responsible or taking a formal step in the disciplinary process, this supervisor seriously weakened the employer's authority to deal with the problem.

So, use the What/Why What/Why formula to begin corrective discipline in a constructive manner and then, if the problem persists, go to the next step of whatever process your state law, written policies and/or union agreements require. Don't procrastinate or try to avoid confrontation. Just go to the next step.

Talk to the individual in private within 24 hours

When I was concerned about an employee's behavior or performance, I tried to talk to them within twenty-four hours. If the incident occurred in the morning, I usually waited until after lunch so I could make notes. If the incident occurred in the afternoon, I usually waited until the next morning to talk with the staff member.

I found that taking time to write down what I needed to say before a corrective discipline interview helped me more clearly identify and communicate the problem to the staff member. I made notes using the What/Why What/Why formula to ensure I discussed everything I intended to say to the employee. Before I started to use the formula, I was more likely to stress over some symptom of the problem instead of the actual problem.

As a new supervisor, I tended to hold back some constructive criticism during the informal interview, probably because I didn't like confrontation or didn't want to hurt someone's feelings. But after my first experience of not saying what I intended to the staff member, I started taking the notes with me to hold myself responsible for telling the whole truth. At the end of the meeting, I gave the original copy of my notes to the employee, and encouraged them to review the notes the next day if they wanted. I also kept a copy of the notes on file.

Do not procrastinate or try to avoid confrontation

By following this practice, I learned the notes helped me say what I needed to say and what employees needed to hear. Understandably, under the stress of corrective discipline, employees often heard what they wanted, or were afraid to hear, instead of what I actually said. Several times during corrective discipline meetings, employees were angry and defensive over what I said, but then in two or three days some came back to say, "Hey! I'm sorry I overreacted, I misunderstood." When I read your notes I realized I can do what you asked." This kind of mature reaction was the exception, however, so be ready to restate and stand firm on what you have said if necessary, so the corrective discipline can be constructive.

Keep thorough written records

Although you can address and resolve most personnel problems after the first step of the constructive disciplinary process, there are times when you have to follow through and terminate an employee. In some cases, former employees will appeal the termination, which may involve personnel officers, union representatives, lawyers, hearing officers, oversight boards, and judges.

Document, document, document. In all cases, throughout the constructive discipline process, it's important you document your meetings and conversations with the employee, your requests for action, and the employee's response. This paper trail is even more important if you ever need to support your decisions and actions during arbitration.

If you follow the What/Why What/Why procedure you should have written notes outlining the problem and why it was important as well as requested changes to the employee's behavior or performance and why they were important. Keep on file copies of every written letter or note from the constructive disciplinary process, including a copy of the notes from the first interview. Also, keep a calendar and save it for several years. Record dates and general topics of personnel action meetings. If you have correctly diagnosed a problem and taken fair and consistent corrective action to solve it, the employee's problem will often become evident during an appeals process.

For example, I once fired a mid-level manager because he was unable to make even simple decisions. He procrastinated about making decisions, and even when he reached a conclusion, he usually changed his mind within a day. After following the first three steps of the corrective discipline process, I told the employee I intended to fire him and offered him the chance to resign because he had enough service time to retire.

I gave him three days to decide and said if I didn't receive a resignation letter by then, I'd send him a termination letter and hold a "good faith and fair dealing" meeting before the effective date. I also told him that during that meeting he could present facts about why I shouldn't fire him. He said he'd think about it.

This employee didn't submit a resignation letter within three days, so I said he'd receive a termination letter that day. He said he'd decided to resign and would submit the resignation letter the following day. By the next day he'd changed his mind, and said I'd have to fire him. I prepared the termination letter that day and gave it to him. The next day he submitted a letter of resignation. I put it in his personnel file, but it was too late. He had already helped me prove my case.

I fired another mid-level manager because he would not delegate and had regular outbursts of anger that made his employees uncomfortable. At meetings he frequently made rude faces, gestures, and comments to staff that certainly disrupted the effectiveness of the meetings.

After this employee was terminated, we went through a fairly lengthy hearing process. He behaved himself fairly well during the hearing—with his attorney sitting right beside him—but the

hearing officer ruled in management's favor. The employee appealed the decision to an oversight board. This time, when his attorney presented the case to the board from a podium at the front of the room, the employee began his usual disruptive behavior in the back of the room. The behavior quickly distracted the board members. It took all my self-control not to look back to watch the former employee. (I didn't want to take the chance that he might stop if he saw me turn around.) Still, I could tell by the way the board members leaned around the attorney to look at the employee that his behavior was disruptive. He helped prove my case.

If you tell the truth, act consistently, establish just cause, and follow due process, you will prevail in resolving problems

The lesson is: if you tell the truth, act consistently, establish just cause, and follow due process, you will prevail in resolving personnel problems even if they go to court. Often, problem employees will recognize the truth and, if they refuse to address their behavior or performance issue, resign. If you have to follow the process through to termination, employees will often demonstrate their problems, particularly behavioral problems, during the appeals process.

Rules for Discipline Problems—Don'ts

As a supervisor, you need to keep in mind your behavior and actions when addressing personnel problems. Don't ignore or violate written policies or act inconsistently, and don't bring your bad behavior to the office during the disciplinary process. Remember, corrective discipline is supposed to be constructive, and to be constructive you have to act in a calm, non-threatening, and fair manner.

Don't act in a fit of temper—Never keep resentment bottled up

Supervisors make two common mistakes when an employee's behavior angers them. Some hold their anger inside then tell themselves they'll straighten the employee out later, only to procrastinate until the problem no longer seems important enough to deal with. Other supervisors blow up and show their anger so strongly they overwhelm and usually embarrass their employees and themselves.

If you procrastinate and don't address the issue quickly, your employees won't know how seriously concerned you are about their behavior or performance, so the problem will probably come up again. Then when you do raise the issue, the employee can rightly respond somewhat indignantly: "If this is such a big deal, why didn't you just tell me before?" This puts you on the defensive instead of positively providing constructive discipline to the employee.

If you blow up, the employee probably won't get the coaching they need from you to improve their behavior or performance. And, they may become so defensive they won't hear or accept the actual message. I witnessed at least one supervisor who blew up one day and invariably felt guilty about his anger the next day. On several occasions, he actually went to the employee and tried to overcompensate for his bad behavior by offering the staff member a raise or some other inappropriate appeasement.

Don't argue with the employee

During corrective disciplinary meetings, no matter at what level, do not argue with the employee. People under stress are prone to make excuses, blame others, or claim other staff are doing the same or worse things and getting away with it. I tried to listen to all this at least once to be sure I understood all the facts. If you determine an employee is making invalid excuses or unjustifiably blaming other staff members, your response consistently should be: "Right now we are talking about you and your behavior (performance), and you need to work on that. Let management worry about your other concerns."

Don't gossip, brag, or discuss other employees

As a supervisor, you are legally required to keep your employees' performance or behavior issues and your corrective actions confidential. You absolutely must not gossip about other employees' personal problems, and you absolutely cannot brag about how strongly you are taking action or how you solved a problem.

But even when you keep issues and problems confidential, you'll likely experience some troublesome employees who, after a corrective discipline meeting, will tell other employees their version of the issues you discussed with them. These employees try to make sure staff tell their version of the conversation to others, no matter how misleading. This won't feel fair to you and may, for at least a short time, prejudice other employees against you for taking corrective action. However, be confident that, if your corrective action is justified and done fairly, (in many cases this will be defined by due process and just cause), time and truth will be on your side.

Every time I had to fire an employee, the positive change in the workplace from having the problem employee gone demonstrated to virtually every other employee that the action I took was appropriate. I'm still on friendly speaking terms with several employees whom I fired, because I had just cause and used due process. I continued to speak to them and call them by name while remaining firm and consistent on needed changes in their behavior or productivity. They may never agree with me, but they respect the way I handled the process.

Never impose a general restriction on all staff when there is a specific problem with only one employee

If one employee acts inappropriately, do not criticize the entire staff. Early in my experience, I supervised a work unit in a building that didn't have an employee break room. To compensate, management allowed staff to leave the building and go to nearby cafes. Before long, I realized one employee was taking more time than was appropriate, so I decided to address the issue at a staff meeting the next day.

At the end of the staff meeting, I expressed my concern about the extended length of coffee breaks. I said I didn't want staff members to abuse the privilege of going out or I'd have to eliminate it. When the meeting adjourned, staff were quieter than usual leaving the room. As I left, the one employee who had been loitering on coffee breaks came up to me and said, "I'm glad you expressed your concern. I've been feeling guilty about how long my breaks are taking, but now that I know everyone was doing it I feel a lot better."

As he walked away, I was struck by the fact that I had managed to demoralize the rest of the staff, who had done nothing wrong, while making the guilty party feel better. I realized I'd threatened to take a privilege away from a lot of dedicated staff because I didn't have the courage or good sense to address the problem directly with the problem employee. Do not make the same mistake I did.

Be careful not to expect more from junior, low-paid employees than from senior, high-paid employees

Occasionally, I'm called in as a consultant to work with managers on personnel issues. In one case, I wasn't in the office very long before I realized the standards of performance and conduct for clerical and technical employees differed greatly from those for management employees.

When developing performance standards, it's important not to expect more from junior staff than senior staff. It's one thing to create preferential policies based on seniority, such as getting first choice on the vacation schedule. But it's entirely another to allow management employees to take longer breaks or come to work late, while you tightly control the length of other employees' breaks and office hours. Policies that indicate some employees are more important than others will almost certainly create personnel issues, such as low morale and increased turnover.

Once I was asked to temporarily supervise a large agency where mid-level managers were dealing quickly and harshly with staff for minor infractions, such as taking long bathroom breaks, while managers were drinking on the job. Upper management ignored the drinking and allowed them to be abusive to clerks. Again, morale was low and turnover was high, because there was such an obvious degree of unfairness in how management dealt with personnel problems.

Don't try to diagnose personal problems
Human resource professionals generally agree that if you supervise employees with performance problems you believe are caused by external factors, don't personally intervene. These factors may include alcohol abuse or mental illness.

Once I took on a new job and inherited a workplace formerly run by a domineering, autocratic management system. In that organization, the supervisor hadn't provided opportunities for staff to think and act independently, didn't recognize them for their achievements, and didn't encourage them to take personal responsibility for their knowledge, skills, and behaviors. So when I became the manager, staff weren't used to making suggestions, let alone decisions. Some employees rejoiced and thrived in this more positive environment, some did not.

Work within your disciplinary process and stick to work-related performance and behavioral issues

One supervisor, in particular, suddenly started drinking alcohol excessively, even at work. He felt uncomfortable with my management style and failed to move forward on several projects until I intervened to provide more direction. In at least one case, one of his employees had to take over a project because he could not be decisive.

I started into the constructive discipline process and expected him to admit what seemed like an obvious alcohol problem. He didn't admit anything, so I pressed him about appearing to be drunk. He claimed he was taking prescription drugs, so I sent him home and told him to work with his doctor to regulate his prescriptions. When he came back to work his erratic behavior continued. I moved to the next corrective discipline step and requested he see an alcohol abuse counselor. I even insisted on going with him. While we were there, he insisted that, although he occasionally had a sip or two of wine, he really did not drink. Soon after, I caught him drinking at work, and told to go home and not return until he had undergone long-term alcohol abuse treatment. Instead of seeking treatment, he went home and apparently drank enough alcohol to put him into a coma. He died within a few days.

What I learned from this situation is to work within your corrective disciplinary process and stick to work-related performance or behavioral issues. Wait for an employee to bring up any secondary factors that may affect their ability to perform the job. When a staff member broaches the subject, then refer them to an employee assistance program or other medical or counseling services.

Words of Advice

Finally, words of advice to those of you who might believe you're being "nice" by not addressing personnel problems. I think by now it's clear that following an established constructive disciplinary process is crucial. You can't transform a workplace and help create committed, competent employees, without identifying and constructively resolving behavioral and performance issues without delay.

If you don't quickly address a personnel problem and move professionally through the established disciplinary process, you deny the problem employee, other staff, and the work unit the opportunity for continuous growth and improvement. Without the benefit of a constructive disciplinary process, the staff member may not have any chance of career stability let alone promotion. By addressing the problem, you may even help some employees realize they aren't really happy in their current jobs and need to change.

You're also not doing your staff any favors if you let a problem fester. It's not fair to expect other employees to pick up the slack for an unproductive employee because you are trying to be "nice" or "understanding." And it's definitely not "nice" to subject good employees to inappropriate behavior because you are avoiding a difficult job responsibility. Again, don't procrastinate, just address the problem constructively and be responsible to both your quality employees and the problem employee.

Chapter 6
The Rules of Delegation

When you delegate, make sure to give staff enough direction to get the job done well and on time without holding too much control.

Delegation is the golden rule of management. There's no question that successful delegation can take more time and effort at first, but in the long run, it's usually a better use of your time to hand over certain tasks when it's not crucial you complete them yourself. You not only improve your productivity, by focusing on your most important tasks, but you show your staff you trust them, which increases their commitment and productivity.

Optimum Delegation

To achieve optimum delegation, you need to identify appropriate staff to complete the projects and provide clear instructions so staff understand what you expect in terms of product, quality, and timeliness. As much as possible, let staff figure out how to accomplish the project. Allow them to bring their personal experiences and qualifications to the project, and provide them the responsibility and authority to grow professionally by completing it.

Provide clear instructions

When you delegate, make sure to give staff enough direction to get the job done well and on time without holding too much control. As a supervisor, you need to provide staff members with clear guidelines that:

- describe the project
- define staff responsibilities and accountabilities
- set performance standards for quality of the work
- set due dates for project completion and interim review.

It's important you're clear about the "what" and the "when" and even the "why" of a project, but try to leave the "how" to accomplish it to staff. Remember, the best employees, ones with commitment and initiative, may come back with suggested improvements to the "what" and "when."

If you don't occasionally feel a little concerned about not being enough in control, you're probably not delegating enough or are over controlling. When you delegate to employees you know are competent and responsible, stretch your trust in them by giving them some decision-making authority within workplace policy and your instructions. Staff should feel some sense of independence and personal responsibility.

You also need to provide clear guidelines about what you expect of staff in terms of minimum standards of excellence, such as "must meet federal standards," and set due dates for project completion. In addition, set interim in dates for staff members to check in with you to make sure they're making progress and will complete the project on time. This is especially true for larger projects.

In addition, set timelines and communication requirements, weekly meetings for example, to allow you to stop or redirect a project if an employee makes a mistake. If this happens, your requirements should be clear enough that you can use the mistake as a teaching tool without being concerned the project will fail. Also, make sure you redirect the work without anger if the employee has been making a sincere effort.

Optimum delegation, which leaves employees some authority and responsibility, will result in staff development. Consequently, staff will be more productive with less supervision and you will have more time to do leader activities so the upward spiral can start speeding up.

Delegate by area of responsibility

It's tempting, and often seems easier, for a supervisor to delegate an important project to an employee who is particularly competent, responsive, or fast. But you should delegate the project to the staff member whose normal area of expertise, based on their job description, relates to the project. If you delegate a project to an employee outside of their usual area of expertise, it hampers staff development. So your goal should be to develop the less effective or slower employee's skills instead of continually turning to another staff member who is already more effective. The only way to ensure the slower, less-experienced, or less-effective employee improves is to insist they develop their skills now, and demand excellence. If you don't help, you'll have the same problem the next time an "important" project comes up. And if you don't train the underachiever, you'll punish more competent employees by over-burdening them with work less-competent staff should be doing.

Delegate projects to the staff member whose normal area of expertise relates to the project

If it turns out that, even with training, the less-experienced or less-effective employee just can't do the job, it's time to start the constructive discipline process. Then a year from now, you won't have the same weakness in your work unit. You're not holding up your responsibility to the unit if you don't address these kinds of issues.

Delegate big jobs to a task force

When a problem seems too big to solve, break it into small problems, and delegate the responsibility to various staff members. If that means building a multi-dimensional task force, keep in mind it's more difficult to delegate to a group than to an individual.

The first time I tried to assign a project to a task force, it didn't go smoothly. After about two meetings, the task force leader came to me and asked if I would attend a meeting to help the team find its focus. Eventually they got on track, but I learned that delegating to a group required even more structure than delegating to an individual.

After that, when I delegated to a team I followed a process to make sure my guidelines were clear and the team could succeed on their own. First, I wrote a memo describing the task force's goal. Then I designated a leader, talked through the project and desired outcomes with them, and asked them to develop a draft work plan as a "charge to the task force." Once we agreed on specific language describing what the task force should accomplish, I sent the plan to all then staff I planned to assign to the team. And I attended the task force's first meeting to make sure members believed the work plan was appropriate and understood what they were being asked to accomplish.

The first few times I assigned work to a task force, I was surprised at how often, even with what seemed like clear direction to me, some members wanted to expand the work or avoid some part of it. I often found myself saying, "Yes I want you to do both A and B," and "No I do not want you to do D. I do not want to do D until we can do C, which we can't do without new budget authority." These conversations often seemed to me like they should be unnecessary. But inevitably, if I didn't take the time to provide written instructions and attend an organizational meeting, the task force would flounder.

Never set a due date you can't respond to

When you set due dates for staff and expect them to complete them on time, make sure you're available to review and discuss the work product when the due date arrives. You'll only demoralize staff if you set due dates and then are not available.

I was once asked to prepare a contract by Friday, and my supervisor left me with the impression he felt it imperative that I present a draft of the contract to him by Thursday afternoon, so we could negotiate the final agreement on Friday. I worked steadily, late into the night, for two days, only to learn Thursday morning the supervisor had called in to say he was going golfing for the next few days. After that, I took his deadlines less seriously. A good supervisor wants their staff to meet deadlines and schedules time to review and respond to the work product.

A close associate of mine used to tell his employees that if they were ever going to miss a deadline, they better warn him well before the deadline occurred. He didn't believe poor planning or procrastination were acceptable excuses for missing a deadline. On the other hand, he always planned his work so he could review and act on projects quickly when staff submitted them to him.

Delegation Problems

As you've, hopefully, learned by now, delegation is a key skill in helping you develop competent, committed employees and transform a workplace. Over the years, I've observed a few mistakes supervisors have made when delegating projects to staff and so I developed a few rules to help other supervisors avoid these problems.

Delegate—Do not abdicate or control

Delegate by setting standards in terms of project goals, quality, and timeliness, but you are too controlling if you require competent employees to check in with you on every detail. On the other hand, if you don't provide clear guidelines to staff and make time for project review, you're abdicating your responsibility as a supervisor.

Avoid upward delegation

Resist employee efforts to get you to do their work or solve their problems for them.

Avoid a broken chain of command

Don't delegate work to any employee you don't directly supervise. It's important you assign work to staff members down through the "chain of command," so the appropriate supervisor controls their staff's workload and holds them responsible for quality and timely work. If you go around the supervisor, you undermine their authority and credibility.

Stop any employee revolt

Stop any revolt from an employee who attempts to get by on the job without making a responsible and timely effort to complete a job or meet a deadline. Also stop any employee attempts to get their way by threatening or bullying you or other staff.

Avoid workload runaway

Make sure you have enough staff to accomplish the assigned projects within the required timelines.

CHAPTER 7
IN-BASKET EXERCISES

If you remember your purpose as a supervisor is to develop staff, you'll strengthen your organization and increase its capacity to provide good service and be effective and efficient, and thus, profitable.

The previous chapters provide tools to help you make decisions, develop structures, and assist staff in taking more personal responsibility for their work and the work environment. Now it's time to apply what you've learned.

This chapter presents a hypothetical management scenario and a series of memos that illustrate various personnel and delegation issues. The memos provide an opportunity for you to practice assessing the kinds of issues supervisors typically encounter in their day-to-day work.

Management Scenario

Imagine you are the regional manager at the Home Health Care Services of Montana Company, based in Helena. On Monday of this week, October 25th, you learned the manager of the Missoula office, which you oversee, was hospitalized and now plans to retire without returning to work. Today, Wednesday November 3rd, the assistant manager of that office called and said he was resigning immediately. The reason he gave was that earlier in the week you said you could not simply appoint him as manager or even guarantee what the future management structure of that office would look like.

You've been concerned about latent morale problems in the Missoula office, anyway, and believe there may be too many managers for such a small office. You don't know the three current supervisors well enough to put them in charge. Unfortunately, you're committed to represent the company at an international symposium the week of November 7th, so you need to go to Missoula immediately to set up an interim supervisory solution. You schedule your arrival at the office to meet with staff on Friday November 5th at 2 p.m.

During the meeting, you explain you'll be gone the next week but will return as manager November 15. You ask staff to carry on as if the manager were on vacation. During the meeting, staff members tell you they're waiting for direction from the assistant manager on some issues, so you agree to go through his in-box to move the issues forward. This is important to ensure the office meets new home health care outreach and services grant program obligations, which include taking new applications and providing new home health care services starting in January.

Your immediate tasks are to: go through the management in-boxes you inherited, organize the work to be done, and set deadlines to accomplish the work on time. Because you'll be out of the office for a week, you need to delegate everything to keep the office on schedule for the upcoming changes.

To make decisions about how you should delegate the work, and what due dates to set, you may want to review the organizational chart and current calendar before starting work on the in-basket exercises.

Missoula Home Health Care Services Office Organizational Chart

	Bob Batter *Manager*	
John Jones *Asst. Manager*		
Pat Perkins RN *Supervisor*	**Norman Noon** *Supervisor*	**Lisa Long** *Supervisor*
Bill Damon LPN	**Mike White** *Eligibility Tech*	**Edith Samson** *Billing*
Rachel Hunt LPN	**Christy Jones** *Eligibility Tech*	**Barb Billings** *Accounts Payable*
Jean Johns LPN	**Ed Roberts** *Eligibility Tech*	
Amy Horseman LPN		
Averill Merrill LPN		

Pat Perkins, RN, supervises the Nursing and Direct Client Services Group; Norman Noon, the Client Enrollment and Eligibility Assessment Group; and Lisa Long, the Administrative Services Group. For this exercise, consider them peers at the management level.

As you use the calendar, remember you'll be out of the office from Friday the 5th until Monday the 15th.

NOVEMBER

SUN	MON	TUES	WED	THUR	FRI	SAT
	1	2	3	4	5	6
7	8	9	10	11	12	13
14	15	16	17	18	19	20
21	22	23	24	25	26	27
28	29	30				

Memo Exercises

Your job now is to read through the memos and respond to the issues as if you were the acting manager until a new manager can be hired. Watch for violations of the rules of delegation as you read. Then write your suggested action to the memo on the bottom of each page. My suggested actions follow each memo. They provide workable alternatives to your actions, but not necessarily the only alternatives. My suggestions might be similar to or different from yours, but will allow you to reflect on the value of different approaches. You need to bring your own style and values to the job.

For some memos, I also provide a summary discussion focused on how well the existing management team followed the rules of delegation and how their actions affected the organization. This discussion is meant to highlight patterns of behavior and management practices to help you determine the effectiveness of past management practices. Does the workplace culture represent an upward spiral or a downward spiral? I'll discuss this more later.

Now, to maximize your understanding of the scene you're entering and optimize your effectiveness in completing these exercises, reread the hypothetical scenario.

Memo 1

Home Health Care Services of Montana Company Headquarters
Helena, Montana

November 3

TO: Bob Batter, Office Manager
FROM: Company Headquarters

Our new Home Health Care Outreach and Services grant for low-income seniors who want to stay in their own homes is about to begin. Your office should be ready to take applications starting December 10th. Our federal granting agency will begin advertising the program on November 15th.

There are some differences in the federal requirements for program enrollment than for all other services we provide. All local area office managers will be expected to meet in Helena at company headquarters, Room 209, at 9:00 a.m. on November 19th to discuss the differences. You should be ready to present and discuss your local area office's work plan for supplementing the federal agency's statewide advertising with area-specific outreach, and for assisting seniors with the application process.

Note: You find this memo in John Jones' in-basket with no note of instruction or delegation from Bob Batter, the manager. What action would you take?

Your Suggested Action

_____

_____

_____

_____

My Suggested Action

This is a simple delegation issue. You should delegate this task to Norman Noon, supervisor of client enrollment and eligibility assessment review. The decision on how much direction to give Norman depends on your knowledge of his skills and abilities. If you knew he had a history of good and timely work, you probably would need only to ask him to prepare the information and have it to you by a date before the November 19th meeting.

Because you don't know his work history, it probably would be wise to ask him to meet with you at a certain time, such as 9:00 a.m. on November 16th to present a draft of his work plan for outreach and application assistance. You also might ask him to have an example of any similar work plan the office has implemented on your desk when you return on Monday November 15th, so you can review it before your meeting the next day.

Memo 2
Missoula Home Health Care Services Office
Missoula, Montana

TO: John, Assistant Manager
FROM: Bob, Manager

Here is a potential public relations problem. I think this guy has a protest march scheduled for next month.
Take care of this will you?

Memo 2 Attachment
American Indian Family Association (AIFA)
Missoula, Montana
October 25

Bob Batter, Manager
Missoula Home Health Care Services Office
1400 Yellowstone Drive
Missoula, MT 59801

Dear Mr. Batter,
Please accept this letter as an expression of the Board of Director's of the American Indian Family Association's (AIFA) concern about how many Indian people will be served under your special Medicare grant for home health care services to Indian people. I would like to remind you that the Indian community comprises fifteen percent of Missoula's population. We believe your office assisted only five percent of our people last year.

We would like to meet with you on November 9th to discuss this issue in greater detail. I hope you will come to our offices that day for our discussion. We look forward to meeting with you.

Sincerely,
Nat Bull Runs
Chairman AIFA

NB: as

Your Suggested Action

_____

_____

_____

_____

_____

_____

My Suggested Action

Again, you should probably delegate drafting a response to the AIFA letter to Norman Noon. Ask him to bring information on the percentage of the Medicare population as a whole that can be served with available funds, compared to the percentage of the Indian population that receives assistance when he meets with you on the 16th. This sets a standard of performance that ensures you receive the information you need in a timely manner to appropriately educate and reassure the American Indian Family Association. You would also want to ask Norman to call chairman Bull Runs and arrange a more convenient date for the meeting.

Summary Discussion—Delegate, Don't Abdicate

This memo demonstrates another example of Bob Batter's abdication of responsibility as a manager. His standard response to any management issue is to send it off to John Jones, assistant manager, with no direction. He doesn't assign due dates, require John to brief him to ensure the project has been accomplished, or set standards for measuring when the job has been completed. He simply hands the issue off and apparently forgets about it.

Bob has abdicated his responsibility because he is not maintaining any control through his delegation. He also is not allowing John or other staff to benefit from his experience and knowledge. This type of manager often gives away all their influence, only to be angry when things don't go well. The anger is then demoralizing to the staff person who is the victim of this abdication because they are overwhelmed by trying to do a job while guessing what the manager's expectations will be. And after working hard, that person is often frustrated by having been second-guessed and criticized without the benefit of receiving any guidance, direction or assistance.

Memo 3
Missoula Home Health Care Services Office
Missoula, Montana

November 2

TO: John Jones, Assistant Manager
FROM: Norman Noon, Supervisor, Client Enrollment
         and Eligibility Assessment

I just returned from our state office in Helena where a staff person told me she'd heard the new federal grant program for outreach would be delayed until the congressional budget was revised after the first of the year. I'm concerned the program will be canceled. And because my staff are so busy, I'm tempted not to follow through on implementation planning. Do you think that would be alright?

Your Suggested Action

_____

_____

_____

_____

My Suggested Action

My first inclination would be to throw this memo in the garbage. If I did respond, I would probably send Norman a hand-written note saying I didn't want to react to unverified speculation, so he should assume the program will start on time. I want to be ready on time even if the program is eventually postponed.

Memo 4

Missoula Home Health Care Services Office
Missoula, Montana

November 2

TO: John Jones, Assistant Manager
FROM: Lisa Long, Supervisor, Administrative Services

I have been trying for a month to find out what an old-2005 is. I thought that surely a mistake had been made and that it must be one of the other group's regular reporting forms, but neither Pat nor Norman have ever heard of it. Have you any ideas?

Memo 4 - Attachment

Montana Department of Human Services
Helena, Montana

October 5

TO: Lisa Long, Supervisor, Administrative Services
FROM: Montana Department of Human Services

As you know, your company's statewide grant for home health care services under Medicare requires that you submit monthly service reports in the old-2005 format for the quarter preceding the start of the grant to establish your service experience and competency. Beginning with the October report, all old-2005s will be submitted by the 10th of each month rather than quarterly so we can build the required data base. Please send your reports electronically, and mail five signed paper copies to our office as well. Make sure all five copies are clear and reproducible. Remember, we cannot approve your new grant unless all required financial, service, and demographic reports have been submitted and approved.

Your Suggested Action

_____

_____

_____

_____

_____

_____

My Suggested Action

Lisa Long's memo is not one I'd be pleased to find in my in-basket, especially so close to a deadline for submitting reports. If there were evidence Lisa had made a sincere effort to track this form down and had provided me some detail about her effort in a more-timely manner, I would be more accepting. At this point, I would probably respond that I expected our office to file reports immediately and meet the filing deadline in the future. I also would request a list of the employees Lisa had called or a copy of any correspondence she sent or received that had failed to identify the source of the report on my desk by the time I returned on the 15th. And I would request Lisa send me an email by close of business on Monday November 8, explaining her plan to track down and file the required report.

Summary Discussion—Employee Revolt

This memo is an example of what I call employee revolt. Supervisor Lisa Long claimed to have looked for a newly required report but could not find it. It is irresponsible for an employee to come back to a supervisor so close to a due date and claim they have made a valid effort. If Long had made a valid effort, and not procrastinated, she would have been able to express her concern to me early enough so I could successfully re-direct her efforts. Of course, there might occasionally be a true emergency, a natural disaster, a power outage, or a coordination problem with a worker outside your employee's control. As a general rule, however, you should not allow an employee to come to you at the last minute and tell you they will miss a deadline.

Memo 5

Missoula Home Health Care Services Office
Missoula, Montana

October 28

TO: John Jones, Assistant Manager
FROM: Norman Noon, Supervisor, Client Enrollment
        and Eligibility Assessment

Would you help me resolve a problem in my group? As you suggested, we started a new appointment schedule for clients to avoid the long waiting times in the lobby. The system would be effective except for the tremendous volume of phone calls we receive from many senior citizens confused about the new Medicare drug insurance. Even with appointments, we have been unable to avoid the long waits while the eligibility techs answer the phone calls.

I am concerned the problem will get worse when the feds begin the new recruitment advertising later this month. Do you have any suggestions about what we can do?

Your Suggested Action

_____

_____

_____

_____

_____

_____

_____

My Suggested Action

This memo, by itself, might be viewed as a note from a supervisor feeling overwhelmed who needs you to help him take a deep breath and take time to consider options. But viewed along with Norman's other memos, this correspondence indicates a pattern of upward delegation.

I would, of course, immediately wonder what ideas Norman has or might develop to solve his problem. With a staff person who behaves like Norman, it's important to require them to develop their own recommendations before asking you to solve their problems. I would send the memo back to Norman suggesting he meet with his staff to get their ideas and then, if he still needed help, to schedule a meeting to talk with you about the recommendations.

Memo 6
Missoula Home Health Care Services Office
Missoula, Montana

November 2

TO: John Jones, Assistant Manager
FROM: Lisa Long, Supervisor, Administrative Services

I am very frustrated and angry with Edith Samson. She is frequently at least an hour late for work and often absent, especially on Mondays and Fridays. As I told Bob in my memo last month, when she is here she is often a good employee in terms of dealing with the public, but she also has occasional temper tantrums, which are always directed at other staff members.

Her erratic schedule makes it impossible for other staff to stay on schedule with their eligibility determinations. Because Bob didn't respond to my last memo, I hope you will end this frustration and terminate her effective immediately.

Your Suggested Action

_____

_____

_____

_____

_____

_____

_____

My Suggested Action

Here is another memo with no record of manager Bob Batter's involvement. Lisa Long refers to a memo, which she apparently sent to Bob Batter last month, that provides no specific information about what constructive action Bob might have taken to correct Edith's attendance. It may be that Bob just procrastinated because he didn't want to face a difficult decision, or maybe Lisa is using Bob's absence to try to get permission to take an action she knows he would not support.

It certainly might be true that a constructive discipline policy exists in the organization, but Lisa has been too impatient to follow the appropriate steps. It also could be that personal animosity exists between Lisa and Edith, and that Edith has a valid medical reason for her attendance problems.

And, of course, maybe Lisa has talked to Edith over and over without taking any intermediate steps in the constructive discipline process, such as sending a warning letter to demonstrate the seriousness of the issue. If so, Lisa may have sent entirely the wrong message about the seriousness of the attendance issues.

All these uncertainties mean you reply to Lisa with a request for more information. It's also probably wise to list your questions so she can be prepared to answer them when you meet with her. Be sure to set a due date.

Memo 7

> John
> Would you handle this?
> Company headquarters doesn't seem to understand the problems we have here.
> Bob

Memo 7 - Attachment

Home Health Care Services of Montana Company Headquarters
Helena, Montana

October 27

TO: Bob Batter
FROM: Office of the Vice-President Customer Relations Office

Month after month our office receives more complaints about your office than about the rest of the state combined because of how long it takes you to schedule appointments for people wishing to apply for assistance through Home Health Care Services Company. We are certainly losing customers because of your office's inefficiency.

Please send me a report detailing the number of claims you processed for the months of September and October, the average length of time for each application to be approved, and an up-to-date priority list of waiting applicants. We need to turn this performance around before the new grant program begins.

cc: Regional Manager

Your Suggested Action

_____

_____

_____

_____

_____

My Suggested Action

You should delegate Norman Noon to draft a reply to the Customer Relations Office. Indicate you expect him to provide ways to improve the approval process in the reply. You might suggest he call other local area offices with similar requirements, and ask how they deal with their workload. Provide him with a due date and standards for the quality of the response.

This memo appears to relate to an earlier memo from Norman asking you for suggestions on how to solve his claims handling problems. This most-recent memo verifies the need for Norman to once again assess his work group's procedures. And, for sure, you want to get his suggestions for your response as the acting manager.

As I've discussed, once again Bob Batter is abdicating his responsibility for managing the office. He doesn't provide John with any due date or quality standards, and doesn't ask to review the memo sent to company headquarters or be briefed about its contents and possible ramifications for the Missoula office.

Memo 8

Missoula Home Health Care Services Office
Missoula, Montana

November 1

TO: John Jones, Assistant Manager
FROM: Pat Perkins, Supervisor, Nursing and Direct Client Services

As you know, November 9th is the deadline for submitting employees' names for participation in the Outstanding Employee's Recognition and Career Development Program. I am still unable to make a decision in my group between Bill Damon, Rachel Hunt, and Jean Johns. All three LPNs have worked long enough for the company to qualify for the program.

Rachel wants to participate in the program very badly, but her performance record does not warrant such a recommendation. She is certainly motivated, but I just don't think our company would benefit from her participation in the program. Bill and Jean have almost identical performance, and I feel both could benefit from the training. Jean seems uninterested in participating, so my inclination is to choose Bill. However, because Jean is Native American I don't want to be seen as being prejudice. What do you want me to do?

Your Suggested Action

_____

_____

_____

_____

_____

My Suggested Action

Once again, a supervisor is asking her supervisor to solve a management problem. At least Pat provides some background and a tentative recommendation. There is, however, no evidence that Pat has conducted regular performance appraisals of Rachel that include Pat's goals for improved performance. There is also no clear evidence from Jean that she is uninterested.

I would probably be somewhat directive here and tell Pat I needed to see Rachel's performance appraisals before disqualifying her. I would also make it clear that anyone with a good performance appraisal should be given the opportunity to state their interest in participating in the program with a written note. Then I would ask Pat to find out about upcoming sessions of the program, so the office could send other candidates. Finally, I would ask Pat to create a consistent approach for selecting candidates. It could be by seniority or by drawing straws, but it would have to be a method employees would see as fair. It also would be good to put the draft policy in writing and let the employees have a chance to comment on the process before it is established as policy.

Memo 9

Missoula Home Health Care Services Office
Missoula, Montana

October 28

TO: John Jones, Assistant Manager
FROM: Norman Noon, Supervisor, Client Enrollment
         and Eligibility Assessment

One of my employees, Christy Jones, is very motivated and anxious to please but doesn't seem able to stay focused on her own work. It seems she is often late with her own work because she's helping other people do their work. I value teamwork and believe her writing skills are helpful to developing other employees' case histories, but then her own eligibility determinations get backlogged. When I talk with her she seems to understand my concerns but continues to help other staff too much. What should I do?

Your Suggested Action

_____

_____

_____

_____

_____

My Suggested Action

In this case, it would be appropriate to suggest Norman talk with the employees Christy is helping. If Norman can demonstrate that her talking to them or doing their work is not appropriate, it's time for him to go to the next step in the constructive discipline process.

With regard to the specific problem this memo addresses: I once hired a young woman into what was her first post-graduation, professional job. It turned out she shared a workspace with a man about ten years older. In addition to being big, he was enthusiastic and for the most part quite likable. His enthusiasm often led to frenetic behavior that could be irritating but also could convince other employees he was very busy and did need help.

Before long, I realized the young woman was working on his projects as much as her own, which often held her work up. After talking to her about it, I realized that, as a young and inexperienced but eager to please employee, she found it difficult to say no to a person who seemed to be her senior.

When I talked to him, I found he believed his work was more important than hers, and because she was a better writer than he was, she should be assigned to help him. I had to work with both employees to get one to back off and the other to be comfortable asserting her independence.

Summary Discussion—Upward Delegation
By now, you should notice the pattern in Norman's memos. He starts each one with "I have a problem" and ends each one with "Have you any suggestions?" In other words, he wants to transfer the responsibility for resolving his problems to you. You have to break this pattern of upward delegation, or you will be frantically trying to do his job and yours, instead of calmly doing your own. In fact, you may end up solving problems Norman's poor performance have caused.

Memo 10

Missoula Home Health Care Services Office
Missoula, Montana

October 31

TO: John Jones, Assistant Manager
FROM: Norman Noon, Supervisor, Client Enrollment
        and Eligibility Assessment

The staff at company headquarters in Helena are causing me a lot of problems. They keep telling customers who complain about how long it takes us to determine eligibility that they should be able to start receiving care immediately. They seem to think we should be able to take an application, determine eligibility, and schedule home health care services that same day.

It's not fair to other applicants to have to deal with the complainers outside the order of their initial inquiry, but headquarters staff disregards fairness to appease anyone who complains. Unless you have other suggestions, I hope you will straighten them out.

Your Suggested Action

_____

_____

_____

_____

_____

_____

_____

My Suggested Action

Here Norman goes again, trying to get you to step in and resolve his problem, with little evidence of what he's done to solve the problem himself. Again, he doesn't provide any suggestions about how to improve service or decrease the number of applicants who complain. You need to send a reply with instructions on how Norman can act more positively and provide more thorough information if he wants you to be involved.

Memo 11

Missoula Home Health Care Services Office
Missoula, Montana

November 2

TO: John Jones, Assistant Manager
FROM: Rachel Hunt, LPN

Please accept this memo within the spirit of improved communication that I intend. I'm only writing this to get your help in getting Lisa Long, my supervisor, to treat all of us more fairly. Her unfairness is affecting my job performance. She continually plays favorites, and Bill Damon, another LPN, is her baseball buddy. They have sons on the same baseball team, and they talk baseball all the time. Because they are always together, Bill hears about the home-health cases first and takes the most interesting assignments. Also, the rest of us have to conduct more home visits than Bill because those two are busy talking about their sons' team. I'm starting to have a bad attitude and often think about asking for a transfer because this is unfair.

Your Suggested Action

_____

_____

_____

_____

_____

_____

My Suggested Action

This memo provides no indication Rachel has talked to Lisa before coming to you. This is an example of a "broken chain of command." For now, you should send this memo directly back to Rachel with a message that she needs to talk to Lisa first. Assure her she is welcome to make an appointment after she has talked with her supervisor and is not satisfied with the result.

You should also make sure Rachel understands you want to build a better team relationship within her work group, and this memo, which bypasses her direct supervisor, can only make the supervisor trust her less. Obviously, Rachel should be trying to build trust with Lisa if she wants to receive more challenging assignments. At some point, however, if Lisa can demonstrate Rachel has had performance problems, I would want to tell her that, normally, better work assignments follow good performance.

Summary Discussion—Staff Performance and Job Assignments

I remember a similar discussion with another new employee. His first assignment was to bring order to a number of customer files that were in bad shape. After several weeks, the employee hadn't managed to get the files into better shape, so I asked him to explain what was taking so long. He said, "Well, it isn't a very important job. Give me an important job and I will do it better." I responded, "This job is important and you can be sure that you have to do this job well before I will give you more responsibility or promote you. What in the world would make you think I would trust you with something more important if I can't trust you to give your best on every job assigned to you? If you can decide this job is not important, how can I trust you to think the next job is important?"

Memo 12

> John,
>
> Take care of this will you?
>
> Bob

Memo 12 - Attachment
Missoula Home Health Care Services Office
Missoula, Montana

TO: John Jones, Assistant Manager
FROM: Pat Perkins, Supervisor, Nursing and Direct Client Services

I have been unable to schedule home health care visits beyond the end of December because I don't have enough information on the budget to determine how much carryover funding will be available next year. Lisa Long says that until we decide how to reimburse staff for personal car use and settle how our computer costs will be charged, she can't notify Norman or me about group expenditures for this year.

As you know, every time the three of us come to a decision as supervisors and present the information to our staff, someone changes their mind and convinces you to bring it up again at the management team meeting. I hope you and Bob come to a final decision on this issue as soon as possible, because I don't know if I can even afford to cover mileage costs to make our current level of home visits for next year. Now, I'm being asked to commit to more visits for next year. So, without this budget information I'm afraid to estimate how many more staff I can afford. We probably should be advertising for staff now, but we need to resolve all this year's expenditures and establish next year's budget first.

cc: Bob Batter, Manager

Your Suggested Action

_____

_____

_____

_____

_____

_____

_____

My Suggested Action

Pat's memo may be the only one in your in-basket that deserves a "Yes I will resolve this soon" response. The problem appears to be a management team that does not have and does not live by a clear decision-making process. You need to schedule a management meeting to discuss and implement a decision-making process that involves staff, but also provides ways the management team can make timely decisions that everyone agrees to support and stick to. Also, note that Bob, the manager, again sent John a memo with no information on due dates, quality standards or a request for a briefing.

Summary Discussion—Decision Making

Supervisor Pat Perkin's memo presents a common management problem: poor decision-making. Pat complains her work group will soon not be able to continue doing their work because no one seems to be able to make a decision, at least not one that will stay made.

I ran into a very similar situation in a regional office for which I was asked to provide technical assistance. I was told early in the work process that management could not make a decision, and problems were discussed over and over for weeks and weeks. Staff were so frustrated that some felt as if management hadn't made a decision for months. By asking a lot of questions, I formed a good picture of what was happening.

Every week, the management team—a group of three supervisors and the regional manager—met. They wanted to be decisive, and by then probably felt guilty, so they tried to make a decision about each issue the first time it appeared on the agenda. After each meeting, the supervisors reported to their work groups on the management team's decision. Usually, at least one work group would have good reasons why the policy decision didn't work well for their particular responsibilities. So that supervisor would go back to the regional manager, outside the management team, and explain why a different decision was needed.

With a high need for decisiveness, the regional manager would agree and change the policy without consulting the other supervisors. The new decision hardly ever pleased the other supervisors or worked well for the other work groups; so, in a week or two they would convince their supervisors to recommend another change. Again, the regional manager would try to be responsive and decisive and grant some exceptions to the new policy, or at least amend the policy enough so that upset staff would feel better. Of course, amending the policy without consulting the rest of the employees usually made them feel like the supervisor was granting preferential treatment. Either this resentment or some other resentment would cause resistance to the policy, if not outright rebellion.

By this time, every work group was frustrated; each one was probably choosing to interpret the policy to their best advantage. They became increasingly resentful because the other work groups were not following the policy the way their group interpreted it. In this unhealthy atmosphere, each supervisor felt a lot of pressure to represent their own staff and to maintain some credibility, so they took little or no responsibility for the management team's decisions.

At the end of this assignment, I recommended that the management team adopt a policy on policies. The staff laughed because it sounded so bureaucratic, but within a few weeks, they found that having the management team create and follow a decision-making process, which was in writing and understood, was very helpful.

Memo 13

Missoula Home Health Care Services Office
Missoula, Montana

TO: John Jones, Assistant Manager
FROM: Barb Billings, Accounts Payable

I have received an offer of a better paying job as a bookkeeper in another company, which would allow me to work from home. The last time I applied for the Administrative Services supervisor job you hired Lisa Long, but I know she plans to quit at the end of the year. So I want to know if I will be given fair consideration for her job this time. If not, I will turn in my notice effective immediately. I must know now to let the other employer know.

Your Suggested Action

_____

_____

_____

_____

_____

_____

_____

My Suggested Action

I'm tempted to return a memo of this type to the staff member with the following quote, "Do not let the door hit you on the way out!" Barb's memo is yet another example of the broken chain of command. My actual response would probably be to send the memo back to Barb with a note saying she should talk to her supervisor, Lisa Long, about her concerns and/or plans. I would be counting on Lisa's recommendation as part of my decision about Barb's potential for promotion. I would probably add that, although I was sure she would receive fair treatment, I could certainly not guarantee her promotion. And I would note that, if any position became available, I would follow the company's written policy or procedure that called for a competitive hiring process. I believe in following written policies and procedures.

Summary Discussion—Employee Revolt

Barb's threat to resign if senior management doesn't agree to give her "fair consideration for the job," a position that is not even open, demonstrates another kind of "employee revolt" and is a form of blackmail. Barb is saying, "You give me what I want or I quit!" No supervisor can give in to this type of threat, and I've never had good results trying to talk an employee into not quitting. Also, you should not allow your employees to think they can threaten and intimidate you, especially if you have consistent written policies and procedures for hiring that are shared with staff.

Memo 14
Home Health Care Services of Montana Company Headquarters
Helena, Montana

November 1

TO: John Jones, Assistant Manager
FROM: Company Headquarters, Training Section

As you know, we have a contract with the Personnel Development Association from Seattle to conduct management skills assessments. Unfortunately, two participants in our November 7th session have canceled, and we need two more staff to participate at this time, or we may have to cancel the course for this month. If possible, I would like to schedule Norman Noon and Pat Perkins for assessments during the week of November 7th. Please let me know by the end of the week if this is possible.

Your Suggested Action

_____

_____

_____

_____

_____

_____

_____

My Suggested Action

You just have to say no. If you agree to send Norman and Pat to the course the week of November 7th, workload runaway would result. There are too many immediate problems and looming deadlines for the new grant program to allow two more key staff members to be gone, especially on such short notice. Staff development is the most important long-range responsibility of a supervisor, but getting the work done well and on time is the immediate challenge for your office. The best process for staff development in this office now would be to establish much better leadership and management practices on site.

Memo 15

Missoula Home Health Care Services Office
Missoula, Montana

TO: John Jones, Assistant Manager
FROM: Lisa Long, Supervisor, Administrative Services

This is really none of my business, but I thought you ought to know that Mike White, one of the eligibility techs in Norman's group, has a tendency to be very rude to the public. When I walk by his office to interact with my staff, I frequently hear him criticize clients who don't have all the documentation needed to complete the eligibility process. Many of our clients are older people who have trouble with their memories. This is part of why they need our help in the first place, so I believe Mike should be more understanding. Anyway, since Norman and I don't get along, I thought I had better let you know.

Your Suggested Action

_____

_____

_____

_____

_____

_____

_____

My Suggested Action

This memo demonstrates another form of a broken chain of command, where one supervisor tattles on an employee of a fellow supervisor. Perhaps the first sentence of this memo is the most important and most-to-the-point comment. Lisa is right. Mike's rudeness should not be her business. It should be Norman's business as Mike's supervisor. If Lisa chooses to express this concern, and she should, because the rudeness should not be allowed to continue, she needs to talk with Norman, not you. He is one of her peers and deserves the courtesy of being spoken to directly.

I would refer Lisa back to Norman, in the hope of them building a better relationship and better customer service. I also would store away the information Lisa provided and try to position myself to discreetly observe Mike's treatment of clients. If I personally observed his rude behavior, I would immediately talk to Norman and have him begin the process of correcting Mike's rude behavior.

Summary Discussion—Chain of Command

This memo represents a significant case of a supervisor breaking the chain of command. In addition to returning the memo to Lisa, you should probably coach her on this. She needs to understand that, as a supervisory peer, she needs to talk with Norman directly and make sure she doesn't ruin her relationship with another member of the management team. You should discuss your responsibility as acting manager to build trust and teamwork among team members, and that coming directly to you can only make Norman feel as if he were tattled on.

Memo 16
Home Health Care Services of Montana Company Headquarters
Helena, Montana

October 25

TO: Bob Batter
FROM: Company Headquarters

We're coming up on the end of the calendar year, and your office still has approximately $50,000 budgeted for temporary help through placement agencies. If you don't need to expend this money for temporary staff at this time, we would like to shift it to other places. Please let me know by November 20th if we can redistribute this money before the end of the year.

Your Suggested Action

_____

_____

_____

_____

_____

_____

_____

My Suggested Action

This memo provides an opportunity for you to bring your management team together to work constructively on a joint project of mutual benefit. You should distribute the memo to all three supervisors with a note saying you'd like them to develop ideas about how to use the money for temporary employees to help with current worker shortages. Your note should set a date, time, and place for the management team to meet and develop a coordinated office plan.

Summary Discussion—Management Assessment

I often present this in-basket exercise in a class setting, where I draw the organizational chart on a piece of paper in front of the class. Then, as each memo is discussed, I draw an arrow from the originator of the memo to the recipient of the memo. As the class looks at the result, and realize all the arrows pointed at one management person, the assistant manager, someone usually asks, "Which manager would it be better to work for?" I usually ask, "Which manager would you want to work for?" Often someone will say, "The Manager! He will let you do whatever you want." And someone else will say, "The Assistant Manager! He will do all your work for you."

These comments always start a discussion, which soon finds the class in agreement that neither manager would be a good one to work for. Not only do they not delegate in a way that will allow staff to benefit from their knowledge or past experience, they don't help staff develop professionally.

Bob Barker, the manager, appears too lazy and uninvolved to add any significant value to work processes or the workplace environment. His approach to management is to pass problems and decisions onto John Jones. But John's stuck in the boss role and is so busy reacting to and helping solve other people's problems he can't add value by acting in the manager and leader roles.

So, the in-basket exercises show not only how a manager can abdicate his responsibility downward, but how supervisors can also abdicate their responsibility through upward delegation by expecting their supervisor, the assistant manager, to solve all their problems and make all their decisions.

It doesn't matter if the reason for consistent upward delegation is the assistant manager's need for control and wish to deal with every issue personally, or he's just not good at delegation. The result is the same: he controls every issue.

What's important to understand is that as long as there is a manager and an assistant manager in the office, they both have to do their jobs without abdicating their authority and responsibility and without controlling staff to the point it stifles staff development and productivity.

As long as the supervisors continue to delegate upward, the workplace can't move into the upward spiral of continuous improvement. If the assistant manager continues to manage in a controlling, reactive manner the job will take charge of him, instead of him taking charge of the job. He won't be able to establish and maintain the structures and processes needed to create a well-managed work place, with an Upward Spiral.

In addition, if the supervisors continue to upward delegate, they won't grow professionally. The assistant manager needs to stop allowing this behavior by requiring the supervisors to think for themselves. They should only come to him when they can present options for him to consider and have done the research needed to answer detailed questions about each option. If you require the supervisors to put that much thought into each problem before they seek your help, they soon will be solving most of their problems independently. This will allow the assistant manager to move out of the boss role and into the manager and leader roles.

This office is definitely stuck in a downward spiral. Both managers and supervisors need to learn and practice the rules of delegation if they want to help start the upward spiral in their workplace.

Conclusion—The Upside-Down Triangle

Remember the organizational chart at the beginning of the practice exercise? Like most organizational charts, it resembles a triangle where the boss is always at the top—because they're considered the most important member of the organization—and the customer service staff are at the bottom because they're considered less important; they have less decision-making responsibility and authority.

The problem with this view of an organizational chart is that if we placed customers on the chart, they'd be at the very bottom of the triangle, which implies they're less important than any staff member, but particularly less important than management.

I believe it's important for management to view the organizational chart triangle upside-down so staff who provide customer service appear more important than the manager, and customers appears most important of all because they're at the top. I hope my views on staff development have convinced you it is in your own best interest to make staff development an everyday job responsibility. It's also in the customer's best interest for the staff to have good knowledge, a calm confidence, and the ability to act independently but with good judgment.

As you go to work each day as a supervisor you should be determined to make each staff member the best employee they can be. View your job as supporting your customer service staff in their effort to serve the customer. If you work with computer software and hardware staff (or personnel, legal, or fiscal staff) your primary concern should be to facilitate customer service. Sure, it's important to look for ways to cut costs or make your reports easier for management to read, but you should always consider the impact of your decisions on your staffs' ability to respond to customers. If you remember your purpose, as management, is to develop your staff, you'll strengthen your organization and increase its capacity to provide good service and be effective and efficient, and thus, profitable.

If you help staff members develop better skills and abilities, take more personal responsibility for their work, and act more independently, you'll gain respect and be a stronger more effective leader. Even if you become owner or president of the company, never allow yourself to think you are the most important person in the organization, and never expect your staff to serve you more than they serve customers.

APPENDIX
T's MOTTOS AND RULES FOR SUPERVISORS

Motto One:
Take charge of your job – instead of letting your job
be in charge of you.

Motto Two:
Your most important long-range responsibility
is staff development.

Motto Three:
A problem employee now means there's a
personnel problem. A problem employee a year from now
means there's a management problem.

Motto Four:
Be effective and efficient.

MOTTO ONE:
TAKE CHARGE OF YOUR JOB – INSTEAD OF LETTING YOUR JOB BE IN CHARGE OF YOU

- Do not do the work! Develop and manage systems that ensure the work is done well and on time.
- Maintain a sense of urgency – the work is important – but absolutely avoid a sense of panic. (Good decisions are made overnight; bad decisions are made under pressure.)
- Be predictable. Keep the expectations of the people you work with in line with reality.
- Put your policies in writing and live by them consistently. Especially:
  - Hiring Process
  - Budget Process
  - Decision (policy-making) Process
- Develop work plans for every definable work unit.
- Have regular informational meetings among work units or peers that must coordinate their work.

- Never set a due date you cannot respond to.
- Keep a regular calendar of all your meetings. Whenever possible, pre-schedule the meeting at least a day in advance and prepare an agenda.
- Use the chain of command. Avoid going around other supervisors, but keep the friendly communication lines open with everyone in the agency.
- When a problem seems too big to solve, break it into small problems and delegate the responsibility for solving them to various individuals.

MOTTO TWO:
YOUR MOST IMPORTANT LONG-RANGE RESPONSIBILITY IS STAFF DEVELOPMENT.

- Never criticize another worker in public.
- Avoid upward delegation.
- Tell people what they are doing right . . . early and often! Positive reinforcement is the most effective method of improving staff.
- In hiring, make sure your interview measures the skills that will be needed for the job.
- Do regular, job-related evaluations and provide constructive criticism in every evaluation.
- Delegate everything. If you think you cannot delegate something because you can do it better, you are too insecure to supervise.
- Delegate everything. If you think you cannot delegate because it will take too long to teach your staff how to do a job, you are too selfish to be a supervisor.
- Keep the size of your staff slightly smaller than the size staff think is optimum. People perform better when they are busy.

MOTTO THREE:
A PROBLEM EMPLOYEE NOW MEANS THERE'S A PERSONNEL PROBLEM. A PROBLEM EMPLOYEE A YEAR FROM NOW MEANS THERE'S A MANAGEMENT PROBLEM.

- Tell employees four things during constructive discipline interviews:
  1. What about their performance is a problem
  2. Why it is a problem
  3. What performance you want instead
  4. Why it is important.
- Never keep resentment bottled up. Express it, but not until your initial anger has passed. As a general rule, wait no more or less than 24 hours.
- Never impose a general restriction when there is a specific problem. If one employee acts inappropriately, talk to that individual employee. Do not criticize the entire staff.
- Be careful not to expect more from junior, low-paid employees than from senior, high-paid ones.
- In situations where constructive discipline is needed in a personnel problem, start dealing with the most senior employee first, unless a subordinate's problem is very much more serious.

MOTTO FOUR:
BE EFFECTIVE AND EFFICIENT

- Responsiveness to the public always comes first, but accurate and complete paperwork is what keeps businesses open or programs available to the public.
- Never surprise someone with bad news in a letter. Whenever possible, make a personal phone call or hold

a personal meeting to give people bad news before the letter arrives.

- Do what you say you'll do, say what you said you'd say, and say it when you said you would. Say what you mean and mean what you say.
- Learn every employee's name and speak every day.

Notes

Notes

_____

_____

_____

_____

_____

_____

_____

_____

_____

_____

_____

_____

_____

_____

_____

_____

_____

_____

_____

_____

_____

32236616R00086

Made in the USA
San Bernardino, CA
31 March 2016